GLOBETROTTER™

Trave

D1589533

MALTA

BRIAN RICHARDS

NEW
HOLLAND

NEW
HOLLAND

★★★ Highly recommended
★★ Recommended
★ See if you can

Fifth edition published in 2008
by New Holland Publishers (UK) Ltd
London • Cape Town • Sydney • Auckland

10 9 8 7 6 5 4 3 2 1

website: www.newhollandpublishers.com

Garfield House, 86 Edgware Road
London W2 2EA, United Kingdom

80 McKenzie Street
Cape Town 8001, South Africa

Unit 1, 66 Gibbes Street, Chatswood
NSW 2067, Australia

218 Lake Road, Northcote,
Auckland, New Zealand

Distributed in the USA by
The Globe Pequot Press, Connecticut

Keep us Current
Information in travel guides is apt to change, which is
why we regularly update our guides. We'd be grateful
to receive feedback if you've noted something we should
include in our updates. If you have new information,
please share it with us by writing to the Publishing
Manager, Globetrotter, at the office nearest to you
(addresses on this page). The most significant contribution
to each new edition will receive a free copy of the
updated guide.

This guidebook has been written by independent authors
and updaters. The information therein represents their

impartial opinion, and neither they nor the publishers
accept payment in return for including in the book or
writing more favourable reviews of any of the establishments. Whilst every effort has been made to ensure that
this guidebook is as accurate and up to date as possible,
please be aware that the facts quoted are subject to
change, particularly the price of food, transport and
accommodation. The Publisher accepts no responsibility
or liability for any loss, injury or inconvenience incurred
by readers or travellers using this guide.

Publishing Manager: Thea Grobbelaar
DTP Cartographic Manager: Genené Hart
Editors: Carla Zietsman, Alicha van Reenen,
Melany McCallum
Picture Researchers: Shavonne Govender, Emily Hedges
Design and DTP: Nicole Bannister, Lyndall Hamilton
Cartographers: Lauren Fick, Reneé Spocter,
Nicole Bannister
Compiler/Verifier: Elaine Fick
Reproduction by Resolution (Cape Town) and Hirt & Carter
(Pty) Ltd, Cape Town.
Printed and bound by Times Offset (M) Sdn. Bhd., Malaysia.

Dedication:
To my wife Sandra, as enthusiastic a visitor to Malta over
the past 25 years as myself, and daughter Claire.

Acknowledgements:
The publisher and author gratefully acknowledge the gener-
ous assistance during the compilation of this book of Air
Malta; Belleair Holidays; Corinthia Group of Companies;
Malta Tourist Office, London; Malta Tourism Authority.

Photographic Credits:
John Johnston, page 110.
Mary Evans Picture Library, pages 14, 15, 18, 19.
Paul Murphy, pages 8, 10, 12, 16, 65 (top), 70, 82 (top), 83.
Brian Richards, pages 7, 9, 11, 20, 23, 24, 25, 26, 27, 28,
29, 34, 35, 37, 38, 39, 40, 41, 42, 43, 45, 46, 48, 50, 56,
60, 61, 62, 63, 64, 65 (bottom), 66, 68, 76, 80 (bottom), 82
(bottom), 91, 92, 93, 94, 101, 106, 109, 111, 112 (top), 113
(top), 114 (top), 116, 117 (right), 118, 119, 120.
Photo Library/Index Stock/Photo Access, front cover.
Robert Harding Picture Library, title page, pages 4, 6, 13,
17, 22, 30, 33, 36, 44, 52, 54, 58, 71, 72, 74, 75, 78, 80
top, 84, 86, 88, 96, 99, 100, 102, 104, 108, 112 (bottom),
114 (bottom), 115, 117 (left).

Cover: The picturesque fishing port in Marsaxlokk.
Title page: A Maltese woman in national dress, with one of
the islands' lively luzzu fishing boats.

CONTENTS

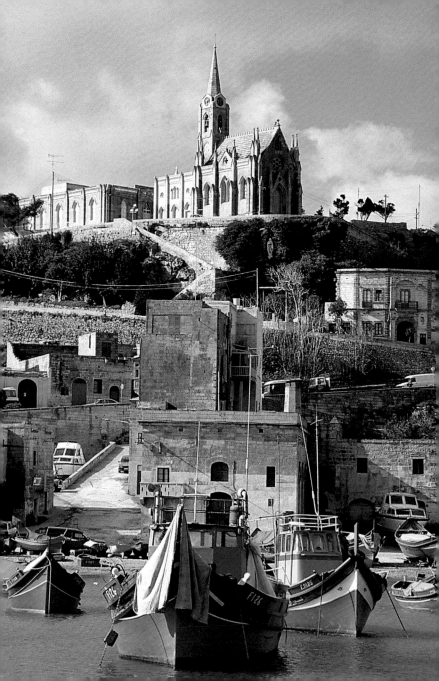

1
Introducing
Malta

Rugged limestone outcrops rising out of the glittering Mediterranean Sea, the Maltese islands are a compact and fascinating blend of history, holidays and friendly small-island hospitality. Malta's colourful past ranges from its earliest inhabitants, who built temples on the islands some 6500 years ago, to the arrival of crusading knights in the Middle Ages and the full brunt of World War II hostilities four centuries later. Added to the best climate in southern Europe, it helps attract more than a million tourists to the islands each year.

The islands are made for sightseeing. History beckons in every town and village, in the wealth of palaces, churches and fortifications that have survived down the centuries. High on every visitor's sightseeing list is the fortified capital **Valletta**. Rising in imposing grandeur from **Grand Harbour**, it is the focal point of urban Malta, which stretches from the resorts of **Sliema** and **St Julian's** to the historical **Three Cities**, and is home to 90% of the islands' population.

The ancient walled city of **Mdina** dominates the centre of the island, an area characterized by small towns and villages, each with its own impressive church. In the south are ancient temples and small fishing resorts, while to the north is the tourist development sprawled around **St Paul's Bay** and Malta's half-dozen or so sandy beaches.

Across the Comino Channel lies the smaller, greener island of **Gozo** and between them tiny **Comino**. Both are popular and attractive getaways for the holiday-maker.

MEDITERRANEAN SEA

TOP ATTRACTIONS

*** **Valletta:** centuries of history within the capital's high ramparts.
*** **Mdina:** medieval walled city of narrow streets and tight alleyways.
*** **Gozo:** spend a day on Malta's green sister isle.
** **Harbour cruise:** for unforgettable aspects of Valletta and the Three Cities.
** **St Julian's:** dine alfresco by the bay as the sun goes down.
* **Marsaxlokk:** fishing harbour packed with brightly painted *luzzu* boats.

Opposite: *Mġarr harbour in Gozo, a classic scene of harbour, historic fortifications and church spire.*

THE LAND

• The Maltese islands lie in the Mediterranean Sea 93km (58 miles) south of Sicily, 368km (230 miles) north of Tripoli and 288km (180 miles) east of Tunis.
• Malta measures 27km (17 miles) by 14.5km (9 miles), with an area of 246km² (95 sq miles).
• Gozo is 15km (9.5 miles) by 7km (4 miles) – an area of 67km² (26 sq miles). Comino is 2.7km² (1 sq mile).
• The shoreline of Malta is 137km (86 miles) long; Gozo's is 43km (27 miles).
• The highest point in the islands is 253m (829ft), southeast of Dingli village in Malta.
• The population of the islands is 390,000.

Malta is both the name of the nation and of the largest of the Maltese islands; Gozo is 8km (5 miles) to the north-west and midway between them is Comino. The island group, which also includes uninhabited Filfla and Cominotto, extends for 45km (28 miles) from northwest to southeast in the centre of the Mediterranean basin.

The islands offer contrasting scenery. Malta largely comprises a limestone plateau that slopes gently from high southern cliffs to the heavily indented northern coast. **Gozo** is blessed with an underlying layer of blue clay that helps to conserve precious rainwater and makes it more fertile. Tiny **Comino** is barren in the extreme.

There are no mountains or rivers in Malta. On higher ground, outcrops of hard coralline **limestone**, most of which has been eroded away, contribute towards the larger island's rugged and semi-arid appearance. Lower down, rough limestone walls bound small enclosures of reddish-brown soil which, despite the annual summer drought, yield a surprisingly wide variety of crops.

Cliffs rising above 250m (800ft) characterize Malta's southern shore – for most of its length there is no way down. Midway along the opposite coast are the impres-

sive inlets of Grand Harbour, with its offshoot creeks, and Marsamxett Harbour. Between the built-up areas the shoreline is rocky. Malta's **beaches** are in the far north, where stretches of golden sand fill the bays either side of Marfa Ridge.

Gozo, a quarter Malta's size, has the same geological structure but varies in character. Flat-capped hills supporting many of the island's villages rise above the green valleys that separate them. This is the garden island, supplying the islands with much of their fruit and vegetable produce.

The Sea

The sea around the Maltese islands is as clean and clear as anywhere in the Mediterranean. It is pleasant to bathe in, excellent for scuba diving and snorkelling and kindly accommodating to a wide array of water sports.

The best **dive sites** are off the steep southern cliffs of both Malta and Gozo, where underwater visibility is mostly between 6 and 20m (20 to 66ft), but can be 40m (132ft) or more. Diving is good year-round, with conditions exceptional between June and October when the sea's surface temperature tops 21°C (70°F).

Bathing off the rocky foreshore is generally safe – flags in the resorts warn of dangerous currents – and the warm water is sometimes at its best in the evening after the beaches have emptied. The smooth rock foreshore at Sliema is a popular spot for diving into the sea. Around the resorts there are plenty of places with boats, canoes and other water-sports equipment for hire and sheltered bays in which to **sail**, **windsurf** and **waterski.** For those wishing to keep their feet dry, **boat trips** operate around the islands and to Comino's spectacular Blue Lagoon, where even the most committed landlubber will be tempted to take a dip. Other fascinating trips explore the subterranean world by glass-panelled underwater safari boat and submarine.

Malta puts its **seawater** to good practical use. Since the mid-1980s, it has established a series of reverse osmosis seawater conversion plants around its coastline; they now fulfil more than half the Maltese islands' freshwater needs and have cured the once-acute water shortage problems that dogged the country.

Above: *Rugged limestone cliffs at Għar Ħasan on the south coast.*
Opposite: *The expanse of Mellieħa Bay in the north.*

MALTA	J	F	M	A	M	J	J	A	S	O	N	D
AVERAGE TEMP. °C	13	13	14	16	19	25	26	26	24	20	18	14
AVERAGE TEMP. °F	55	55	57	61	66	78	79	79	76	69	64	58
Hours of Sun Daily	5	6	7	8	10	12	13	12	9	7	6	5
RAINFALL mm	83	55	40	22	10	2	0	0	30	83	87	97
RAINFALL in	3	2	2	1	0.5	0	0	0	1	3	3	4
Days of Rainfall	14	11	9	6	3	1	0	0	3	9	11	14
Sea Temp. °C	15	14	15	16	18	21	24	25	24	22	19	17
Sea Temp. °F	59	58	59	61	64	70	75	77	75	72	66	62

Climate

Malta's climate is just about the best the Mediterranean can offer – a hot summer sun blazes from a cloudless sky and the mild winter days have sufficient rain to green up the rocky landscape. The country's appeal as a year-round holiday destination owes much to the weather pattern. With one of Europe's best sunshine records, Malta is ideal both for a seaside 'burn' and a culturally motivated short break out of season.

In July and August the thermometer regularly hits the upper 30s Celsius (mid-90s Fahrenheit). The average for those months is a gloriously warm 26°C (79°F). Take care with sunbathing – remember that Malta is further south than parts of North Africa and that the sun deserves more respect than usual. Take sunglasses, too – the strong sun reflects off Malta's light-coloured buildings with real intensity. Overall the sunshine quota is generous, with a daily average of around 12 hours in high summer and even five hours a day in deepest winter.

Below: *Crowded beach umbrellas provide a colourful contrast to sand and sky at Golden Bay.*

While the wind blows mostly from the northwest (the wind is known as the *majjistral* in winter, when it blows strongest), the northeasterly *grigal* and northerly *tramuntana* can cause the odd storm from late summer onwards. Better known is the *sirocco* or *xlokk*, the warm and humid southeasterly wind that blows off the Sahara and can roughen up the sea along the southern shores. Malta's rainfall averages around 500mm (20in) annually, but can be half that figure in a drought year or double it if the winter months are particularly wet.

Flora and Fauna

Malta packs a surprising diversity of produce into the small fields packed between dry rubble walls that crisscross its countryside. Terraced cultivation of the hillsides and careful irrigation of low-lying arable land also help maximize the country's agricultural output. On Gozo, known as 'Malta's kitchen', the presence of water-retaining blue clay soil means the island remains greener than its larger sister and is thus able to provide much of the islands' food requirements.

Crops reared in the thin soil covering include potatoes, tomatoes, onions, capers, wheat, maize, melons and sesame – plus animal fodder for winter. Small plantations of olives, figs, carobs, oranges and lemons exist, but grapes are the main fruit grown. These are mostly used to make the local wine. Fields are fallow in summer, when the sun parches all growth; by mid-autumn the ground is greener. Winter's vegetation is richer than you could ever imagine in high summer, while spring bursts forth in a bright array of roadside flowers and glorious fields of colour.

Wildlife in Malta and Gozo is scarce and restricted to lizards, geckos, the occasional snake and those birds, mostly migratory, fortunate enough not to have been trapped or blasted from the sky by hunters. The reservoirs of Chadwick Lakes near Rabat and the Għadira Nature Reserve at Mellieħa Bay are the only bird habitats, providing visiting ornithologists with a variety of sightings in spring and early autumn.

Wild flowers abound in autumn, winter and spring – more than 600 varieties that carpet the valleys, ravines and ridges of the Maltese islands with a blaze of colour. There are few **trees**, however. Most of the forest that once covered Malta was destroyed long ago to provide wood for ships and buildings and only the trees of Buskett Gardens survive.

Above: *A poppy field colours the countryside above Salina Bay.*

MALTA'S ENDANGERED VISITORS

The Maltese islands' position midway between Europe and North Africa makes them a convenient touchdown point for birds which breed in northern Europe and winter further south. Some birds make Malta their winter home and become even more dependent on the efforts of Birdlife Malta (the former Malta Ornithological Society) to protect them from hunters. An estimated 25,000 hunters trap small songbirds and sell them in cages, and up to a million migratory birds are shot or trapped in large nets each year.

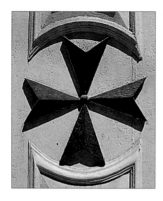

Above: *Symbol of an island republic: the familiar Maltese Cross was introduced by the Knights in the mid-16th century.*

HISTORY IN BRIEF

Long before man arrived, the Maltese islands were joined to both Europe and Africa. The first inhabitants probably came about 7000 years ago from Sicily, which is only 93km (58 miles) away. These were early **Neolithic** people who farmed and reared animals, used stone implements, made pottery and eked out an existence in isolated communities.

Later generations were the builders of ancient temples and tombs cut from rock, awe-inspiring handiwork dating from before 2000BC which can still be seen throughout Malta and Gozo. Successive incursions of Bronze Age colonists followed before the arrival of **Phoenician** civilization in Malta around the 9th century BC.

The Phoenicians traded with the western Mediterranean and initially sought refuge in Malta's natural harbours. They brought prosperity to the islands, which subsequently came under the influence of their descendants, the **Carthaginians** – who, from their base in Tunis, gave Malta strategic importance for the first time. With Rome's influence in southern Italy growing, conflict between the **Romans** and Carthaginians was inevitable. In the firing line, Malta became a military base in the **First Punic War** (262–242BC), when it was sacked by the Romans. Though the Carthaginians regained control, Malta was seized again by the Romans in the **Second Punic War** (218BC) and stayed tied to Rome.

Malta prospered under Roman rule and important towns developed where Mdina and Victoria now stand. However, Malta retained many Phoenician influences and opinion is still divided over whether Malta's name originates in the Phoenician *malat*, meaning port, or the Roman *meli*, meaning honey. It was under the Romans that one of the most important happenings in Maltese history occurred – the shipwreck of St Paul the Apostle on Malta in AD60 and the conversion of the islands to Christianity.

With the decline of the Roman Empire in the fifth century, Malta found new masters in the **Byzantines**.

THE MALTESE CROSS

The eight-pointed cross – now known as the Maltese Cross because of its long association with the island – was introduced to Malta as the emblem of the **Knights of St John**. The eight points represent the eight Beatitudes; the four arms stand for the four virtues – prudence, temperance, fortitude and justice. It shouldn't be confused with the George Cross which appears on Malta's flag.

HISTORICAL CALENDAR

5000–3750BC Malta populated by Neolithic farmers from Sicily.
3750–2000BC Great period of temple building that includes Tarxien and Ġgantija.
800–218BC Malta under the Phoenicians and Carthaginians.
218BC Romans take Malta in second Punic War.
AD60 St Paul shipwrecked.
5th/6th centuries Roman power in decline; Byzantines rule Malta.
AD870 Arabs conquer Malta.
1090 Roger the Norman captures Malta from the Arabs.
1282 After periods of German and French domination, Malta comes under Aragon (Spain).
1530 The Knights of the Order of St John of Jerusalem arrive in Malta, a gift to the Order by Charles V of Spain.
1565 Great Siege of Malta.
1566 Valletta prepared as Knights' new capital.
1571 Valletta replaces Birgu as capital.
1798 Malta falls to the French under Napoleon. The Knights are ordered from the islands.
1800 The British move in; the French are evicted.
1814 Malta becomes a British Crown Colony.
1921 Self-government gives Malta responsibility for its own domestic affairs.
1940 First air raid on Malta in World War II.
1942 Malta is awarded the George Cross after 154 consecutive days of bombing.
1964 Malta independent.
1974 Malta becomes a republic within the Commonwealth.
1979 British forces leave Malta.
2004 Malta is one of 10 new member nations to join the European Union.

In AD870 the **Arabs** conquered Malta from their base in Sicily and held the island for more than two centuries. Their influence still shows in the Maltese language spoken today and the many place names of Arab origin.

When Count Roger the Norman led an invasion from his kingdom in Sicily in 1090 and restored Christianity under **Norman** rule, the Arabs were allowed to remain for a while. As Sicily switched hands, so did Malta; western European influences increasingly prevailed and by 1282 Malta found itself administered by the **Spanish**.

In 1530, Holy Roman Emperor Charles V granted Malta to the **Knights of the Order of St John of Jerusalem**; their stay as masters of Malta lasted until the 1798 capitulation to Napoleon's **French** forces.

In 1800 the **British** assumed control and the 1814 Treaty of Paris confirmed Malta's status under the British crown until the granting of independence in 1964. The Maltese islands, once more of high strategic importance, played a heroic role during World War II in the face of incredible odds which earned them the George Cross. In 1974 Malta became a republic within the Commonwealth and in 2004 it joined the European Union.

Below: *Malta's national flag since the country became independent from Great Britain in 1964.*

Below: *Philippe Villiers de l'Isle Adam, the first Grand Master on Malta.*

The Knights of St John

In 1530 Malta was given by **Charles V**, Holy Roman Emperor and King of Spain and Sicily, to the Knights of the Order of St John of Jerusalem. This powerful chivalric Order had been founded 400 years earlier as the Frères Hospitaliers de St Jean de Jerusalem, a group of monks attached to a hospital which had been set up for pilgrims in Jerusalem.

Their hospitality included providing escorts through the Levant; they became armed and gradually military duties took over. After the successful First Crusade, which ended in 1099, the Knights became a full military order, but still combining soldiering with nursing. Nearly 200 years later, the Order was turned out of the Holy Land by the Moslems and sought refuge in **Cyprus**.

In 1310 the Order left Cyprus for **Rhodes**. Over the next two centuries the Knights of Rhodes, as they were now known, became wealthier and ever more powerful, and built up a navy to defend their shores. It was not powerful enough, though, to overcome the 400-strong Turkish fleet of Suleiman the Magnificent in 1522 and after a six-month siege the Knights were sent packing once more.

For seven difficult years under Grand Master **Philippe Villiers de l'Isle Adam** they sought a new base. A temporary home was secured in Italy and France before the offer of Malta, first made in 1523, was unenthusiasti-cally accepted. The Order was given the Maltese islands, together with Tripoli, in perpetuity for an annual rent of a falcon. After the ideal conditions of Rhodes, Malta was viewed in a poor light.

The Knights found it infertile, unfortified and with too few inhabitants to mount a pre-sentable defensive force.

Early Days in Malta

While the Knights were unsure about Malta, the Maltese received their new tightly disciplined masters with caution; it took a common enemy, the **Turks**, to bring about full conciliation. On arrival in Malta, the Knights found the main settlements to be the fortified city of **Mdina** and the village of **Birgu** by Grand Harbour – they chose Birgu (now Vittoriosa) as their base because it offered mooring for their oared galleys off Grand Harbour. The Grand Master set himself up in Fort St Angelo at the end of the Birgu peninsula.

Vows of the Knights

The Knights, committed to defence of the Church and care of the sick, maintained a secular lifestyle through vows of chastity, obedience and poverty. Additionally, they pledged never to fight against another Christian country, never to gamble or run into debt and never to shrink from battle.

Above: *One of two bronze cannon guarding the cathedral in Mdina.*

To join the Order, a prospective Knight of Justice had to be Catholic, of aristocratic birth and able to provide a dowry – once accepted, he was established for life. Other grades of membership in the Order were Chaplain and serving brothers; two honorary grades, Magistral Knight and Knight of Grace, were bestowed on those who had given outstanding service. When a Knight died, the Order inherited his estate.

The Eight *Langues*

The Knights were split into nationalities, or *langues*, as a measure of convenience in battle. There were eight *langues*, although those of **Auvergne**, **France** and **Provence** would nowadays be regarded as one. Other *langues* were **Aragon**, **Castile**, **England**, **Germany** and **Italy**; the English *langue* lapsed with the Reformation led by King Henry VIII in 1540.

Each *langue* was headquartered in an *auberge*, a hostel with its own accommodation, dining hall (where the food

THE GREATEST LEADER

No Grand Master made a greater impact as head of the Order than Frenchman **Jean Parisot de la Valette**. Born in 1494, he joined the Order aged 20 and became Grand Master in 1557, 27 years after the Knights' arrival in Malta. His first task as head of the Order was to strengthen Malta's defences in anticipation of a Turkish invasion; his greatest hour came with the capitulation of the Turks that ended the Great Siege of 1565. La Valette gave his name to the new fortified capital on Mount Sciberras, inaugurated on 28 March 1566; he died in 1568 and is buried in St John's Co-Cathedral in Valletta.

Above: *The raising of the Great Siege in 1565.*
Opposite: *A depiction of the Turkish invasion.*

The fall of Fort St Elmo to the Turks on 23 June 1565 after 31 days of unbroken siege precipitated savagery unmatched at any stage in the battle. The Turkish commander Mustapha Pasha, having lost 8000 men in taking the fort, ordered the decapitation of several important Knights; the heads were impaled on stakes facing Fort St Angelo and the torsos, nailed to planks, were set adrift in Grand Harbour. Four bodies reached the opposite shore, prompting immediate retaliation from Grand Master La Valette. He ordered the execution of all the Turkish prisoners in Fort St Angelo, loaded the severed heads into cannon and fired them back across Grand Harbour at the Turks in Fort St Elmo.

was reputed to be excellent) and chapel. At first these were in Birgu; when Valletta became the capital, the *langues* moved to larger premises there. At the head of the Order was the **Grand Master**, responsible only to the Pope and elected for life. In all, 28 Grand Masters presided over the Knights in Malta between 1530 and 1798; the longest-serving was **Manuel Pinto de Fonseca** (1741–73), founder of the university.

By the time the Knights had come through the Great Siege of 1565 and made their base in the new capital of Valletta six years later, the Order was being overtaken by progress. The Knights had long ago found ways round their poverty vows and had assembled a fleet of sailing ships to replace their galleys, but these would prove insufficient to take on the sea might of the Mediterranean powers.

In 1798, **Napoleon** ended the Knights' presence on Malta without a shot being fired. The French fleet stopped by on its way to Egypt and issued an ultimatum to the Knights' first German Grand Master, **Ferdinand de Hompesch**. The Order hastily surrendered Malta to the French and within three days had left the island with only their personal belongings, never to return.

The Great Siege
The Knights' reputation as defenders of Christendom and the Maltese islands peaked in a bloody four-month battle with the **Turks** in 1565. It came to be known as the Great Siege, in which 700 Knights and 9000 Maltese held out against Turkey's military might of 30,000 men and an armada of 200 ships sent by the Sultan, **Suleiman the Magnificent**.

The Turks were feared throughout the eastern Mediterranean as aggressors and conquerors, but saw Malta under the Knights as an ever-present threat to their quest for territorial gains in southern Europe. To this end, Gozo was sacked in 1551 and some 6000 inhabitants – almost the entire population – reduced to slavery. Encouraged by this success, the Turks laid plans for a large-scale attack on Malta. It was known by the autumn of 1564 that an invasion was inevitable and in preparation the Knights under Grand Master **Jean Parisot de la Valette** had strengthened Fort St Elmo and Fort St Angelo which guarded Grand Harbour. La Valette's request for European help had been ignored and the Turkish fleet arrived off Malta on 18 May 1565.

The Attack on St Elmo

Target of the Turks' initial assault was Fort St Elmo, which held out for 31 days against repeated attacks before capitulating. The Turks lost 8000 men, including their leader Dragut Rais; some 1500 defenders, including 130 Knights, were killed.

Next the Turks turned on Birgu and Senglea, which had been strengthened by limited reinforcements from Sicily. A great chain slung across the dividing creek kept the invading fleet at bay while defenders in the

> **Diversion to Mdina**
>
> After three months of siege action around Grand Harbour in the summer of 1565, the Turkish commander-in-chief Mustapha Pasha turned his attentions to Mdina. The fortified capital on its rocky bluff could only be taken from the south and with an attack imminent, Mdina's Governor Don Mesquita dreamed up a bold plan to frighten off the invaders. With only a small garrison, he had the peasants and their womenfolk dress in soldiers' uniforms and parade with the troops along the ramparts. The ploy worked. Faced by what they thought was a mighty well-armed garrison, the Turks retreated and Mdina was spared.

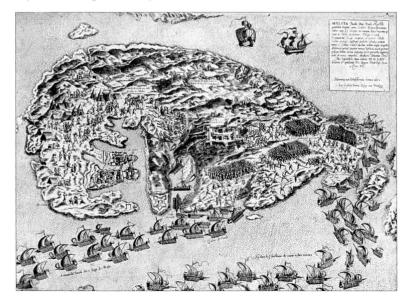

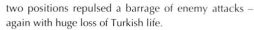

Around Malta you will see everywhere evidence of 179 years of British presence:

• Above every police station door is the classic British police force blue lamp.

• Older telephone boxes and letter boxes are red.

• The few remaining old cars – Ford Anglias, Vauxhall Victors and Morris Minors – were made in Britain.

• Vintage buses carry the painted names of manufacturers such as Leyland, Bedford and AEC, although their true British pedigree is more doubtful.

• Driving, as in Britain, is on the left, and as you do you may find yourself travelling past such establishments as the Coronation Store and the Britannia Bar.

two positions repulsed a barrage of enemy attacks – again with huge loss of Turkish life.

The assault lasted several weeks, but with morale declining in the oppressive heat and disease further decimating their forces, the Turks finally fled for home. Two-thirds of the invasion force had been killed in the conflict between Christian and Muslim.

The French and the British

French control over the Maltese islands was brief but destructive. After the Knights had been sent packing in 1798, Napoleon did away with the privilege of nobility; his forces plundered any spoils left by the Knights and defaced many of the Order's buildings. All manner of restrictions were placed upon the Catholic Church and its property continued to be plundered.

This led to a **revolt** by the Maltese in Mdina which spread rapidly throughout the island. The French complement of 4000 men retreated to the towns around Grand Harbour and stayed there until a **British** blockade under Captain Alexander Ball, aided by the Maltese, forced their surrender in September 1800.

Malta was at first seen by the British as having bargaining value rather than the strategic worth that had been so readily recognized by Napoleon. But the Maltese took to their new masters and, anticipating a return of the exiled Knights under Russian or Neapolitan protection, argued strongly that the islands should become a British colony.

The relationship confirmed by the **Treaty of Paris** in 1814 was to last for 164 years. Malta's value to Britain as a naval base increased throughout the 19th century, aiding territorial expansion

Below: *A blue lamp in evidence at St Paul's Bay police station.*

further east and the Crimean War effort. The opening of the **Suez Canal** in 1869, combined with the development of steamships, gave Malta and Aden dual prominence as coaling stations on the sea route to the Far East.

By the turn of the century, trade growth resulting from the steamship era had left Malta trailing rival Mediterranean ports. Dockyard employment increased during **World War I**, when Malta again played the role of 'nurse of the Mediterranean'; during the conflict, while Maltese signed up with British service units, the islands provided 25,000 beds for the wounded and sick.

In 1921, Malta became self-governing in local matters, leaving Britain to take care of wider issues like foreign policy. But the system failed and in 1930 the constitution was suspended – to be restored two years later and again suspended in 1933. It took the onset of World War II (*see* p. 18) to unite the dissident factions.

After the war, Malta received £30 million from the British government to help rebuild the island and in 1947 self-government was re-established. The mid-1950s saw an imaginative plan to fully integrate Malta with Britain, with Maltese MPs to be returned to Westminster. The plan was, however, rejected in a referendum as the Maltese Church was not keen to join with the Anglican.

On 21 September 1964, Malta achieved **independence**, but chose to maintain ties with Britain. The Queen remained sovereign of the islands and Malta stayed within the Commonwealth. Under the Nationalist government, British forces were to remain in Malta for 10 years in return for £50 million in grants; when **Dom Mintoff**'s Labour party took office in 1971 this was renegotiated and the last British forces in Malta sailed out of Grand Harbour on 31 March 1979. Malta became a republic within the Commonwealth in 1974, the Queen's place as head of state going to a Maltese President, appointed for five years by the House of Representatives.

VICTORIA LINES

A series of fortifications running the length of the high ridge just north of Mosta, built by the British between 1875 and 1885, took the name Victoria Lines in 1897 to mark the diamond jubilee of Queen Victoria. The forts and gun-batteries include Fort Binġemma in the west, Fort Mosta and Targa Battery in the centre and Fort Madliena in the east, all linked by a masonry parapet. By the turn of the century their military value was in question and in 1907 the Victoria Lines were abandoned. The best-preserved section is the Dwejra Lines north of Mdina.

Below: *A panel on the Palace of the Grand Masters in Valletta commemorating the award of the George Cross in 1942.*

Below and opposite:

*Italian publications record
wartime air raids on Malta.*

Malta in World War II

At the outbreak of World War II, Malta was Britain's
most important Mediterranean naval base. As such, it
was to protect west–east supply lines while blocking the
passage between Italy and North Africa. When Mussolini
plunged Italy into the war on 10 June 1940, Malta knew
for sure that it was destined to play a frontline role.
Europe was nine months into the conflict when, on 11
June, Malta suffered its first **air** attack on the dockyard.

At that point, Malta's entire anti-aircraft resources
totalled 42 guns, two dozen searchlights and three
Gloster Gladiator biplanes which had been discovered
in crates and were hurriedly assembled. The
Gladiators, christened *Faith, Hope* and *Charity*, were
matched against 200 Italian aircraft based 100km (60
miles) north in Sicily. On the face of it there was surely
no contest, but by forcing enemy aircraft to bomb from
a greater height, the three small Glosters more than
earned their keep. The Maltese people no longer felt
like a sitting target, and for three long weeks the proud
Gladiators defended Malta's air space alone until
Hurricane support arrived.

In December 1940, the German air force moved into
Sicily to support the Italians and
with 250 aircraft the combined
Axis forces outnumbered Malta's
aerial strike force by four to one.
Meanwhile, German and Italian
submarines maintained a relentless
assault on the supply convoys.

Malta's Darkest Hour

Malta's worst period of the
war was in early 1942, when
the air raids never ceased. In April
alone, 6700 tonnes of bombs
rained down on the island and on
the 15th of that month a special
message from the British king,
George VI, informed the people of

Malta that they had collectively been awarded the **George Cross** for their unyielding bravery. Some relief was forthcoming with a delivery of Spitfires and slowly Maltese air power was built up to 200 aircraft. With a more powerful air combat force, Malta's position strengthened during 1942 and by October, when the British Eighth Army succeeded at **El Alamein**, the Axis threat had been considerably weakened.

Targeting the Convoys

Ultimate control of the central Mediterranean hinged on supply lines and in the early months of 1942 the Allies suffered heavy shipping losses in the Malta-bound convoys. For much of the year the country's civil and military population was reduced to near starvation levels, relying on a communal feeding service and being forced to eat their diminishing animal stocks – not until early in 1943 did the rationing situation improve.

Cost of Malta's War

It took the Allied assault on Sicily in 1943 to effectively end Malta's close involvement in the war. The island acted as a fighter base during the operation to capture Sicily's airfields and once this had been achieved the Axis powers were unable to continue their harassment of shipping in the central Mediterranean. For Malta, three years of war had been intense. The islands had endured some of the most ruthless bombing of World War II and it was primarily because the buildings were of stone that huge sections of the towns were not destroyed by fire. Nearly 1500 Maltese civilians were killed in the air raids.

The clearing-up operation lasted for years. Valletta's bombed seaboard was still rubble into the 1950s and the rebuilding of the towns around Grand Harbour, now collectively known as the Three Cities, took nearly a decade.

THE SANTA MARIA CONVOY

In the summer of 1942, Malta was in dire need of food and fuel to continue its struggle against the Axis powers. As the Maltese prayed to Santa Maria, whose feast day was due on 15 August, Britain sent a convoy of 14 merchant ships under armed escort. As the ships neared Malta they came under massive air and sea attack. Nine merchantmen were sunk; the five remaining included the tanker *Ohio*, with 11,000 tonnes of fuel critical to Malta's survival. On 13 August four vessels limped into Grand Harbour. More prayers were offered to Santa Maria and on the morning of the 15th the *Ohio* reached Malta. The islands were saved and the name of the Santa Maria Convoy became legendary.

The Maltese either loved or hated Dom Mintoff, the former Labour leader and Malta's best-known politician. The Oxford-educated civil engineer and architect served as Prime Minister from 1955–58 and 1971–84; throughout the 1970s his name was synonymous with that of Malta as he maintained non-alignment with the super-powers and distanced himself from the Catholic Church. Mintoff set himself apart on the world stage by demanding commercial aid from various left-wing leaders in preparation for the British military withdrawal in 1979.

Below: *A harbour cruise in Dockyard Creek: tourism provides Malta with more than a quarter of its gross national product.*

GOVERNMENT AND ECONOMY

When independent Malta became a republic on 13 December 1974, economic stability was the priority facing the Labour government of Prime Minister **Dom Mintoff**. Ties with Britain were to be finally severed in March 1979 with the departure of British forces, leaving Malta to seek economic assistance elsewhere.

The British military withdrawal, at the end of an extended defence agreement made at independence in 1964, had a drastic effect on employment in the islands. The job losses were partly offset by widespread **emigration** to Canada and Australia; today as many Maltese live abroad, particularly in Australia, as in the islands themselves.

New Friends for Old

In the mid-1970s, Mintoff declared a policy of strict neutrality, cultivating closer friendships outside Europe with the likes of Russia, China and Libya that gave rise to unease in Europe. But the fears born out of Mintoff's worldly fraternizations proved without foundation – the previous Nationalist government had already pledged its future to Europe through an EEC association agreement, forerunner to Malta's initial application for full **European Union** membership in 1990.

Head-to-head Politics

Participation in Malta's two-party politics is a national pastime. Clubs for **Nationalist** and **Labour** followers proliferate, an indication of the close inter-party rivalry. In each intensely contested general election, the margin of victory is slender.

After three consecutive spells in government, the Labour party found itself

shunted out by the Nationalists in 1987. **Dr Carmelo Mifsud Bonnici**, having replaced the retiring Mintoff as Prime Minister in 1984, was forced out of his Castile office three years later, when **Dr Eddie Fenech-Adami** took over the reins in the House of Representatives. Under the Nationalists, who were re-elected in 1992, again in 1998 after a brief intervening Labour period and in 2003, Malta has taken a firm pro-Europe stance, which culminated in the country joining the European Union on 1 May 2004.

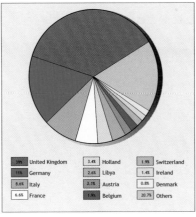

39%	United Kingdom	3.4%	Holland	1.9%	Switzerland
11%	Germany	2.6%	Libya	1.4%	Ireland
8.6%	Italy	2.1%	Austria	0.8%	Denmark
6.6%	France	1.9%	Belgium	20.7%	Others

TOURIST ARRIVALS BY NATIONALITY

Tourism to the Fore

While other Mediterranean holiday destinations have seen their fortunes ebb and flow, Malta's popularity remains high. Visitor numbers remain consistent and the islands welcome more than 1.1 million annually. The **British** love affair with Malta continues after more than 30 years of independence, with around 430,000 visitors from the United Kingdom annually.

Tourism is now Malta's principal industry, providing around 24% of the country's gross national product. The highly impressive **Malta International Airport** terminal, able to handle 2.5 million departing passengers a year, was opened in 1992; two years later the new **cruise ship terminal** below Valletta's bastions received the first of many white-hulled cruise liners.

Shipshape Economy

Shipping continues to play a significant part in the economy, with the Malta Shipyards successfully tendering for servicing and repair work on tankers and container ships plying the Mediterranean. Additionally, the Malta **Freeport** distribution centre in the south of the island is well established as a foreign exchange earner. **Agriculture** also makes a solid contribution, despite the compact nature of Malta and Gozo.

RADIO AND TV

For such a small population, the Maltese people enjoy a vast selection of radio and TV – 13 radio stations at the last count, including local community stations, four local TV stations, 10 Italian TV stations and many more available on cable/satellite. While TVM remains the country's prime TV station, the Italian channels are popular with Maltese viewers – the high-masted TV aerials you see on your travels around the island are needed for tuning in to Italy.

Above: *There's always time for a chat: men catch up on the local gossip in Republic Street, Valletta.*

THE PEOPLE

To the visitor, the locals might all be Maltese, but those born and bred in Gozo will claim they are Gozitan first, Maltese second. There has always been friendly rivalry between the two sets of islanders, with Malta people telling jokes about the 'mean' Gozitans and Gozo folk forever claiming intellectual superiority.

Through the centuries, despite domination by a succession of expansionist-minded invaders, the Maltese have clung steadfastly to their strong insular identity. Gregarious by nature among themselves, they are generally friendly towards visitors, though it will be noticed that waiters and others in the service industry often make little effort to please.

Typically among Latin races, the Maltese are devoted to the **family** and family life. Families are often large and stay closely in touch; in such a small island community parents, brothers, sisters, aunts, uncles and their various offspring all live within a short distance of each other.

As business in Malta tends to be male dominated, women are left to play the traditional home-caring role. It is today's generation of daughters, keen to develop their own careers, who are freeing themselves from the constraints of the past.

Attitudes to **dress** are conventional in Malta, a country of firm social traditions. Visitors should be suitably attired when entering churches to save causing offence. Topless sunbathing is against the law.

Religion

Malta's Roman Catholic roots run deep. The majority of the population is devoutly Catholic and the Church plays a large part in their lives, as is shown by the size of the churches in even the smallest villages. The islands have more than 350 churches, from the

It is said that a dozen Maltese family names are shared by 90% of the population; after a short time in Malta you will be familiar with most of them. Among the most popular surnames are Azzopardi, Borg, Calleja, Camilleri, Caruana, Galea, Gatt, Grech, Pace, Tabona, Vella and Zammit. Maltese families remain close-knit, continuing to live in the same town or village or often the same street. Don't be surprised to see a family gathering of 30 or more enjoying Sunday lunch together in a restaurant.

awesome edifices of St John's Co-Cathedral in Valletta and Xewkija's parish church on Gozo, down to those the size of the tiny chapel on Comino.

With four out of five Maltese regularly attending mass, the need for so many churches is readily apparent. Not all are in permanent use, however – some isolated chapels are unlocked only on feast days. Nearly all services are held in Malti.

Throughout the islands, **Holy Week** has special meaning. Large crowds turn out in towns and villages for the Good Friday processions – those in Rabat, Mosta, Qormi and Żebbuġ are among the largest. Local organizations march slowly at the head of the procession, focal point of which are the life-sized statues depicting the Passion and death of Christ, supported shoulder high by men in hooded white robes. The processions can last for hours and it takes six strong men to carry each of the painted wooden statues, with frequent pauses to rest. People dressed as soldiers and Biblical characters also march to the sombre music. The Easter Sunday procession, by contrast, is more of a parade. Usually led by the local band, it is a much happier occasion, with a statue of the risen Christ carried through the streets to the sound of church bells.

A traditional feature of **Christmas** is the illuminated crib displays, some with moving figures, to be found in several of Malta's village churches.

Craftware

The variety of traditional crafts still practised in Malta and Gozo come packaged in two craft villages – the former airfield site of **Ta' Qali** in Malta and **Ta' Dbiegi** in Gozo. Here you can watch skilled craftsmen in action and buy gold and silver filigree, decorative coloured glassware, ceramics, pottery, Malta stone ornaments in calcite onyx or limestone, wrought ironwork, brass door knockers and wicker furniture. Prices in the craft villages are competitive.

> **SACRED SPOTS**
>
> Malta's religious character shows in the number of shrines dotted about the islands – by the wayside and on street corners; even set in the wall of Valletta's ruined Opera House. Flickering candles in their red see-through holders and fresh flowers are an ever-present reminder of the Maltese people's strong religious convictions. Builders of Malta's old buses often incorporated a small, illuminated shrine behind the driver; some bone-shaking vehicles prominently spread the word that 'Jesus Lives'.

Below: *Colourful Maltese craftware for sale at the market place.*

Specialist **Gozitan** craftwork includes lace napkins, handkerchiefs and tablecloths, and cheap and chunky woollen jumpers and cardigans. Village women sit outside their homes in the cool of a summer's evening, chatting and working away with knitting needles or lace-maker's cushion. Durable hand-woven Malta Weave rugs, tablecloths, bedspreads and soft toys are other good buys.

Watercolours by local artists are also excellent value. Among the most popular artists is **Edwin Galea**, painter both of tranquil island landscapes and all-action sea battles depicting Maltese history from the Great Siege to the present day.

Language

Such is the Maltese familiarity with English that visitors need concern themselves only with the pronunciation of place names. Determined linguists will discover that the Maltese language of Malti, Phoenician-based with Arab modifications and later English and Italian influences, is complex and not the easiest to speak or understand.

The Village *Festa*

To the uninitiated, staccato crackling in the air above and accompanying bursts of thick smoke might imply that one Maltese village has declared war on another.

Opposite: *A statue of the risen Christ is paraded through St Julian's on Easter Sunday.*
Right: *Banners decorate the streets of towns and villages at festa time.*

To everyone else, the aerial explosions mean that another *festa* (festival) is under way. This is the highlight of every parish calendar, a five-day celebration of its patron saint's feast day wrapped round a weekend of non-stop action that successfully blends piousness with wild celebration. The *festa* season kicks off two weeks after Easter with the Feast of **St Publius** in Floriana, and continues through to **September**. Colourful flags and bunting flap in the breeze and statues line the streets during *festa* week.

The parish church is dressed, ornamented and lit up by hundreds of light bulbs for the occasion; inside the saint's statue is adorned with flowers. After the services, crowds follow the statue through the streets. A brass band plays and there is general merrymaking late into the night, culminating in a spectacular firework display which the villagers have saved for all year.

PLACE NAMES

Pronunciation difficulties are caused by accented letters (ċ = ch; ġ = j; ż = ts) and silent letters (għ; h, though aspirated at the end of a word; and q). Other pronunciations are: ħ = h; j = y; x = sh; m = im when an initial letter and followed by a consonant, as in Mdina. You may find yourself having to pronounce the following:

Dwejra (*d'way-rah*)
Ġgantija (*jee-gann-tee-yah*)
Għar Lapsi (*ahr-lapp-see*)
Għar Dalam (*ahr-dall-am*)
Għarb (*ahrb*)
Għasri (*ahs-ree*)
Ħaġar Qim (*ha-jah-eem*)
Lija (*lee-yah*)

Luqa (*loo-ah*)
Marsaxlokk (*mar-sah-shlok*)
Mdina (*im-deen-ah*)
Mġarr (*im-jarr*)
Mnajdra (*im-na-eed-ra*)
Mqabba (*im-ab-ba*)
Msida (*im-see-dah*)
Naxxar (*nash-shar*)
Qala (*ahl-ah*)
Qawra (*ow-rah*)
Qormi (*orr-me*)
Qrendi (*ren-dee*)
Siġġiewi (*sij-jee-e-wee*)
Ta' Ċenċ (*ta chench*)
Tarxien (*tar-she-en*)
Xagħra (*shuh-ra*)
Xewkija (*show-kee-yah*)
Xlendi (*shlen-dee*)
Żebbuġ (*zeb-booj*)
Żejtun (*zay-toon*)
Zurrieq (*zuhr-ree*)

FESTIVALS FOR ALL

• The **Malta Jazz Festival** takes place on the third weekend in July at Ta' Liesse, Valletta and has a reputation for attracting star names.

• At the end of July the **Farsons Great Beer Festival** takes place over 10 days at Ta' Qali Park.

• In early October, the **Birgu Festival** in Vittoriosa alternates with the **Mdina Festival**. Both combine Maltese art, crafts and folklore with pageantry and re-enactments.

• In November, the **International Choir Festival** attracts choirs from throughout Europe.

THE MALTA EXPERIENCE

An established and popular
screen attraction brings history
to life at St Elmo Bastion in
Valetta, where Malta's
fascinating story from
Neolithic times to the
present is told in an ever-
changing kaleidoscope of
images from 44 projectors
complete with sound effects,
accompanied by multilingual
commentary. Presentations of
The Malta Experience take
place hourly from 11:00–
16:00 from Monday to
Friday; from 11:00–13:00 at
weekends and holidays
(11:00–14:00 Oct–Jun).

After a period in the 1970s and 1980s when it was
held in May, **Carnival** in Malta is now firmly established
in the period immediately preceding Lent, to herald the
approaching end of winter and arrival of spring.
Carnival was started by the Knights in the 16th century,
when it was led by the Grand Master; now towns and
villages throughout Malta join in the celebrations with
fancy-dress parades, lavishly decorated floats, folk
dancing and, of course, firework displays. The biggest
and most colourful procession takes place through the
streets of Valletta.

Entertainment

Malta may not be renowned for its dynamic nightlife, but
what there is caters adequately for a wide cross-
section of holiday-makers and includes a **theatre**, **casinos**,
cinemas and **discos**. Most hotels offer entertainment of
some kind, such as sing-along **piano bar**, **cabaret** or
colourful **folk-dancing show**.

If it's loud **music** you're after, head for the neon-
adorned music bars of Paceville and St George's Bay,
thundering out their wild range of dance, house, rap
and reggae offerings. There are some good hi-tech discos
with wall-to-wall lasers and advanced sound systems to
satisfy the most sophisticated boppers. It was not always
thus – as recently as the 1980s, Paceville was still
primarily residential, enlivened by
just a scattering of restaurants.

Below: *A summer
evening's bocci game
at Buġibba. Towns and
villages throughout
Malta have their own
bocci clubs.*

Film buffs have been spoilt for
choice since the expansion of the
Eden Cinemas' Megaplex at St
George's Bay to 17 screens, showing
an interesting blend of brand new
releases and older films – all in
English. Other multiscreen cinema
complexes have sprung up elsewhere
in the island. Be prepared for inces-
sant chatter and popcorn crunching
during the film; also for the sudden
picture fade-out and interval.

The **Manoel Theatre** in Valletta, Malta's cultural hub, stages ballet, opera and concerts by its own symphony orchestra. Plays are performed, but rarely in English. If you fancy a flutter, the Dragonara Casino Barrière at St Julian's grants membership to visitors. Take up the offer – the inside is worth a look.

Sport and Recreation

Malta's menfolk (but very few women) turn out in force on Sunday afternoons for the **trotting** meetings at Marsa, to enjoy the programme of a dozen or so races that takes nearly five hours to complete. Bet on the Tote and then sit in the sun and count your winnings. Admire the grace of movement as up to a dozen impeccably groomed beasts pace twice round the 1000m (⅔ mile) Marsa Race Track; the circuit has been there since 1868. Immediately outside the arena some of the 700 trotters registered with the Malta Racing Club are stabled. Trotting is Malta's most popular spectator sport and regularly attract crowds of up to 4000.

There are plenty of participant sports to occupy the visitor, from **golf** at the par-68, 5017m (5487yd) Royal Malta Golf Club to the **Malta Marathon**, held each February, and **tenpin bowling** at the computerized Eden Super Bowl in St George's Bay. The extensive Marsa Sports Club complex offers weekly or daily membership to visitors and includes **tennis**, **squash**, **billiards** and **swimming** in a freshwater pool. Increasingly, tennis and squash courts are found in hotels, as are **fitness centres**. The informal game of *bocci* – like the French boules but using a combination of balls and coloured wooden blocks – is a national pastime. Soccer is popular in Malta and top foreign teams have a strong following.

> **MALTA'S BEST BEACHES**
>
> • **Mellieħa Bay** is Malta's longest beach, excellent for water sports, safe swimming and sunbathing.
> • **Golden Bay** lives up to its name, with fine yellow sand and a range of water sports.
> • **Għajn Tuffieħa Bay**, next to Golden Bay, is quiet without being secluded and is excellent for bathing.
> • **Gnejna Bay** is popular with the locals – a small beach with limited facilities but offering peace and quiet.
> • **Ramla Bay** is Gozo's main beach, its soft yellow sand packed with sunbathers all through summer.
> • **San Blas Bay** is Gozo's best-kept secret – a tiny beach at the foot of a steep path and strong on solitude.

Below: *Trotting meeting at the Marsa Race Track.*

Malta and Gozo are renowned for their **water sports**. There are several diving schools on the islands and plenty of opportunities for sailing, waterskiing and windsurfing. Maltese teams do well at water polo, which is also a popular spectator sport. **Fishing** is possible either off the rocky foreshore or by arrangement with a local boatman; there are no organized excursions.

Above: *A selection of home-grown Maltese fare.*
Opposite: *Some of the wines produced on Gozo.*

MALTESE SEAFOOD

The Maltese serve fish in many ways – fried, grilled, poached, baked and stuffed, stewed, in a pie and with a variety of tasty sauces. Many restaurants offer a 'fresh fish of the day' – you might see *pixxispad* (swordfish), *acciola* (amberjack), *dentici* (sea bream), *cerna* (grouper), *tunnagg* (tuna), *merluzzo* (red mullet), *dott* (stone bass) and *fanfru* (pilot fish) – plus a Maltese speciality, the *lampuka*, which breeds in the Nile delta and is in season from early Sep until late Nov. Also available are calamari, octopus, lobster and prawns.

Food and Drink

Consider the many foreign influences that have shaped Malta's character and it follows that the country's cuisine will be broad based – vaguely **Mediterranean**, flavoured with **Italian** and a dash of the **British**; possibly with a hint of **Arabian**. Many restaurants steer a culinary course between British and Italian, to satisfy the conservative palates of holiday-makers.

While genuine Maltese dishes appear on wider menus, there are still few restaurants specializing in the traditional cuisine of the islands. Nevertheless, there are many restaurants providing excellent fare, often in a rustic Maltese setting – though it is not necessarily the best for those thinking about their diet. Don't be put off by the sun-faded pictures of food outside.

Locally grown **vegetables** such as green peppers, globe artichokes, aubergines and marrows play a big part in Maltese cuisine. They can be stuffed with anchovies, minced pork or cheese to make a filling meal, possibly accompanied by thick chunks of Malta's excellent crusty **bread**.

Fast food and medium-fast food have long been an established way of dining in Malta. There are dozens of

TRADITIONAL MALTESE DISHES

Aljotta: boiled fish soup with tomatoes and garlic.
Braġoli: or beef olives; thin slices of beef rolled into an olive shape around a mixture of minced ham and pork, bacon, egg and peas.
Fenek: rabbit, simmered country-style in wine, baked or in a stew.
Ġbejna: local cheese made from sheep's or goat's milk, often with peppercorns.
Minestra: a heavy soup with pasta (usually macaroni) and vegetables.
Pastizzi: puff pastry cakes filled with ricotta cheese.
Ravjul (Ravioli): familiar pasta shapes filled with ricotta cheese rather than meat.
Ross il-Forn: baked rice dish with minced pork, beef, bacon, eggs and ricotta cheese.
Soppa tal-armla (Widow's Soup): filling soup with soft cheese, ricotta cheese, eggs, lettuce, peas, carrots and onions.
Stewed octopus: octopus in a sauce of onions, tomatoes, olives and capers.
Swordfish in caper sauce: fried swordfish with a sauce of capers, tomatoes and onions.
Timpana: a golden brown baked macaroni dish with minced beef and pork, eggs, cheese, chicken liver and bacon.
Torta tal-Lampuka (lampuka pie): *lampuka* is a favourite local fish, here accompanied by onions, tomatoes, spinach, olives and capers in flaky pastry.

pizzerias in the resort areas, and several international fast-food chains are now well represented in major centres of population.

That the Maltese have a **sweet tooth** is clear from the huge variety of cream-filled cakes and pastries on sale in kiosks and coffee shops. You cannot fail to notice the sweet aroma of frying *imqaret* (date slices with aniseed) or be surprised by the many varieties of *qubbajt* (nougat) at *festa* occasions. The sweet specialities at Easter are the almond-flavoured iced biscuits called *figolli*. Fresh fruits available include oranges, figs, plums, peaches, grapes and melons.

FRUIT OF THE VINE

Through the introduction of a greater number of quality wines in recent years, Malta is now taken more seriously by wine drinkers. Wines such as Cabernet Sauvignon, Chardonnay, Merlot, Pinot Bianco, Pinot Grigio and Sauvignon Blanc are now found on the supermarket shelves. With Maltese wines, you get what you pay for; wines at the top of the range are good while those lower down, while drinkable, can take some getting used to. Grapes are imported from Sicily and the northern and southern regions of Italy. More adventurous imbibers might try wine from Gozo – powerful stuff with a high alcoholic content that has been known to induce a couple of hours sleep. Local beers like **Cisk** (lager) and **Hopleaf** (pale ale) are good; so is the bittersweet **Kinnie**, a Maltese soft drink now being exported.

2
Valletta

Valletta is a city which has impressed many people down the years. Sir Walter Scott called it 'that splendid town quite like a dream', to Lord Byron it was 'a city built by gentlemen for gentlemen', while Benjamin Disraeli found that Malta's capital 'equals in its noble architecture, even if it does not excel, any capital in Europe . . . that fair Valletta, with its streets of palaces, its picturesque forts and magnificent churches'.

Nowadays Valletta casts its spell over more than a million visitors annually. It cloaks the finger-peninsula of **Mount Sceberras** between Malta's two great harbours – **Marsamxett Harbour** on one side and **Grand Harbour** on the other – at the centre of the island's conurbation.

HISTORY

Valletta owes its defensive character to the **Great Siege** of 1565. It was after the Turks had been repelled at such enormous cost that Grand Master **Jean Parisot de la Valette** decided the Knights should relocate from Birgu into a new fortified city across Grand Harbour which was eventually to bear his name.

The foundation stone was laid with great ceremony on 28 March 1566 by the Grand Master himself. The humbling of Turkish Islam and strengthening of Christianity in the islands encouraged widespread financial support and Pope Pius IV sent his chief engineer, **Francesco Laparelli**, who had designed such a city before the Great Siege, to supervise the work.

MEDITERRANEAN SEA

DON'T MISS

*** St John's Co-Cathedral: Valletta's incomparable church of the Knights.
*** Palace of the Grand Masters: the impressive headquarters of the Knights for more than 200 years.
*** Grand Harbour: see it from Upper Barracca Gardens.
** A walk around the ramparts: a leisurely and informative couple of hours.
** Lascaris War Rooms: nerve centre of the Allies' Mediterranean fleet during World War II.

Opposite: *A street in Valletta, with Grand Harbour at its foot.*

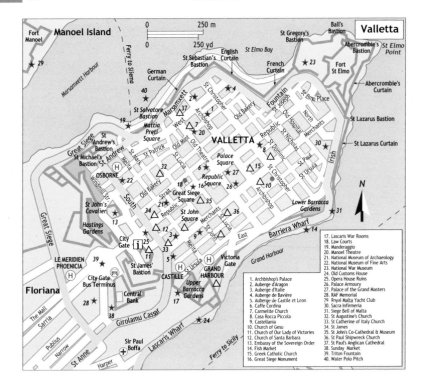

Valletta

1. Archbishop's Palace
2. Auberge d'Aragon
3. Auberge d'Italie
4. Auberge de Bavière
5. Auberge de Castille and Leon
6. Caffe Cordina
7. Carmelite Church
8. Casa Rocca Piccola
9. Castellania
10. Church of Gesu
11. Church of Our Lady of Victories
12. Church of Santa Barbara
13. Embassy of the Sovereign Order
14. Fish Market
15. Greek Catholic Church
16. Great Siege Monument
17. Lascaris War Rooms
18. Law Courts
19. Manderaggio
20. Manoel Theatre
21. National Museum of Archaeology
22. National Museum of Fine Arts
23. National War Museum
24. Old Customs House
25. Opera House Ruins
26. Palace Armoury
27. Palace of the Grand Masters
28. RAF Memorial
29. Royal Malta Yacht Club
30. Sacra Infirmeria
31. Siege Bell of Malta
32. St Augustine's Church
33. St Catherine of Italy Church
34. St James
35. St John's Co-Cathedral & Museum
36. St Paul Shipwreck Church
37. St Paul's Anglican Cathedral
38. Sunday Market
39. Triton Fountain
40. Water Polo Pitch

SCENIC WALKS

A walk around the perimeter of Valletta on the road that follows its defensive curtain wall yields views across Marsamxett Harbour and Grand Harbour without parallel. It is a couple of hours well spent and there are open-air bars for refreshment on the way. The trip can also be done by traditional horse-drawn *karrozzin* – the views are just as good and you may be treated to an informative commentary.

A massive work force of Maltese, Sicilians and foreign slave labour was assembled to build the enormous bastions. On the landward side of the peninsula, a ditch hewn from the rock 1km (⅔ mile) long and 18m (60ft) deep added further protection. Within five years the new capital of Malta was born.

Sadly, La Valette never saw completion of his ideal. He died aged 74 in 1568 and building of the city continued under Italian Grand Master **Pietro del Monte**. When engineer Laparelli returned to the Vatican in 1570, the project was overseen by his Maltese assistant **Gerolamo Cassar**, later to design the fabulous Palace of the Grand Masters, the Co-Cathedral and the Knights' *auberges*. It was in early 1571 that Del Monte decided to move the Knights' headquarters from Birgu to Valletta.

Europe's First New Town

The original ambitious plan for Valletta called for the upper part of barren Mount Sceberras to be flattened and the sloping sides further steepened. But time was critical, money was running short and another Turkish attack was feared. The work never took place, which accounts for the smooth, polished streets of stone steps still found in steeper parts of the city.

Only 1km (⅔ mile) long and 600m wide, Valletta became Europe's first 'new town', designed from the drawing board on a grid pattern. Eight streets run dead straight for most of the peninsula's length, crossed by narrow, stepped side streets which fall away sharply at right-angles towards the two harbours.

The city's clean architectural lines were achieved by strict planning regulations. Houses were of similar design, with no gap between them and with statues at each corner. Incorporated into the plans was space for the Knights' *auberges*, the Palace of the Grand Masters, the hospital and church of the Order. Despite the severe bombing it suffered in World War II, Valletta today remains both an architectural and cultural delight – a place to be revisited often. Few visitors come to Malta without spending some hours in and around the capital, if only to jostle with the locals and tourists at the Sunday morning market beneath the towering bastions.

Nearby, next to City Gate, is the bus terminus packed with its noisy yellow buses (many of Malta's buses range from old to positively ancient) which connect every town and village with the capital. By day there is a bustle of workers, shoppers and strollers; by night Valletta is left to slumber in relatively uninterrupted peace.

In a city best explored on foot, every street holds fascination. Museums, palaces and churches vie for attention with squares and gardens; and at every turn there is a glimpse of harbour between the yellowing façades.

THE FOUNDER OF VALLETTA

The man who gave his name to Valletta, **Jean Parisot de la Valette**, was Grand Master of the Order of St John of Jerusalem from 1557 until his death in 1568. He was a man of immense courage, dedicated to furthering Christendom and destroying the Turks – an objective achieved with the triumph in the Great Siege of 1565. At La Valette's insistence, the Knights remained in Malta thereafter and built the fortified city that was to remain their home until 1798.

Below: *Old yellow buses link Valletta with every town and village.*

Above: *Neptune Court, larger of the two inner courtyards in the Palace of the Grand Masters.*

THE SIGHTS OF VALLETTA

Palace of the Grand Masters ★★★

The most highly prized of Malta's palaces is now the seat of the President and Parliament of the Republic of Malta. Every building of the Knights' era was constructed on a grand scale – and the Grand Masters' Palace exceptionally so. However, its impressive, if unadorned, exterior yields no clues to the artistic treasures within.

The inspiration behind the palace was Malta's supreme architect of the 16th century, Gerolamo Cassar. He shouldered responsibility for the building's design and construction in 1571, once the Knights had decided to transfer their headquarters from Birgu across to the newly completed fortified city of Grand Master La Valette.

The palace had started life two years earlier as a house built for Eustachio del Monte, nephew of Italian Grand Master Pietro del Monte. Impressed by the building's focal position on one of the highest points of Mount Sceberras, Del Monte purchased it for the Knights and commissioned Cassar to turn it into a palace.

It was modified by successive Grand Masters until the Order left Malta in 1798. From 1814 it became the British Governor's official residence; since the mid-1970s its mighty walls have contained the office of the President.

The palace encloses two greenery-adorned courtyards. Leave Palace Square through the left-hand archway into the tranquillity of **Neptune Court**, with its bronze statue of Neptune, said to have been rescued from a fish quay in the 17th century. The smaller **Prince Alfred Court** contains a fascinating four-faced clock of 1745 with Moorish figures that strike the quarter-hour.

GEORGE CROSS ISLAND

A stone panel set in the wall of the Grand Master's Palace on Republic Street commemorates the award of the George Cross to the Maltese people during World War II's darkest days. The citation of King George VI, dated 15 April 1942, read: 'To honour her brave people I award the George Cross to the Island Fortress of Malta to bear witness to a heroism and devotion that will long be famous in history'. The George Cross is now displayed in the National War Museum at Fort St Elmo.

Inside, beside the **marble staircase**, a panel reminds today's visitors of all 28 Grand Masters. Up the stairs are listed Britain's representatives in Malta from 1800 until independence in 1964.

The **Tapestry Room**, formerly the Council Chamber of the Knights, is a magnificent spectacle, with its superb timbered ceiling and set of exquisitely preserved Gobelin tapestries, a gift of Grand Master Ramon Perellos in 1710, which depict mostly imaginary scenes of India, Africa, the Caribbean and South America.

Equally impressive is the Hall of St Michael and St George, also known as the **Throne Room**. Here, too, admire the fine ceiling and the series of Great Siege frescoes painted by Matteo Perez d'Aleccio (1547–1628), believed to have been a pupil of Michelangelo. The decorated gallery opposite the throne is said to have been brought by the Knights when they fled Rhodes.

In the **Hall of the Ambassadors**, in which the Grand Master met envoys, a frieze recalls the Knights' pre-Malta history in the eastern Mediterranean. Canvasses of British royalty add a rather more recent aspect to the **State Dining Room**.

The Armoury **

One of the world's most significant and impressive permanent exhibitions of pre-18th-century weaponry and armour is found in two halls within the palace precincts. The most recent weapons are North European air guns from 1800.

The collection of armour includes an Italian-made half-suit believed to have belonged to Grand Master La Valette, the Italian gold-inlaid suit of French Grand Master Alof de Wignacourt which dates from 1615 and a suit said to have been worn by Grand Master Martino Garzes. A group of armour-clad model Knights stands on parade among the display of guns, swords, rapiers, daggers, pikes, lances and other weapons.

> **ARCHITECT SUPREME**
>
> **Gerolamo Cassar** (1520–86) was Malta's master architect of the 16th century. As assistant to the Pope's engineer Francesco Laparelli, he helped to plan and build Valletta; when Laparelli returned to Italy in 1570, Cassar took charge. His many fine achievements include St John's Co-Cathedral, the Grand Masters' Palace, the *auberges* of the Knights, Our Lady of Victories Church and the original Carmelite Church in the capital. He also designed Verdala Palace.

Below: *Knights on parade in the Armoury. The fine collection of weaponry and armour numbers some 6000 pieces.*

Below: *The Auberge de Castile et Leon houses the Prime Minister's office. The statue is of Maltese writer Manuel Dimech (1860–1921).*

The *Auberges* ★★★

An *auberge* was the main base of a *langue*, or nationality, of the Knights. Originally there were eight of them in the city, but now just five of the Knights' headquarters survive. The *auberges*, mostly designed by Gerolamo Cassar between 1571 and 1590, vary enormously, from the magnificent Castile to the single-storey simplicity of the Auberge d'Aragon.

The **Auberge de Castile et Leon** (the ex-British army headquarters which now houses the Prime Minister's office and is referred to as simply Castile) is one of Malta's finest edifices. It commands the way into the upper city, its Baroque green-shuttered façade dominating Castile Place at the head of the main arteries Merchants Street and St Paul Street.

This was the palace of the Spanish and Portuguese Knights, built originally in Renaissance style by Cassar in 1574 but restyled in 1744 by Maltese architect Domenico Cachia under Grand Master Manuel Pinto de Fonseca. Pinto's bust, with carved banners, arms and Grand Master's crest, is prominent above the cannon-flanked steps at the entrance.

A hundred paces down Merchants Street is Cassar's **Auberge d'Italie**, headquarters of the Italian Knights and now the Ministry of Tourism and Culture. Built in 1574, it was enlarged in 1683 for Grand Master Gregorio Carafa, whose bust appears above the door, and at one time housed the Law Courts.

Nearby on Republic Street, the Cassar-inspired **Auberge de Provence**, built in 1575, now houses the National Museum of Archaeology (*see* p. 43). With its façade of Doric and Ionic columns, it was the mansion of France's Provence *langue* and under British rule was home to the Union Club, focal point of Maltese society. Two other French *auberges*, the **Auberge de France** and **Auberge d'Auvergne**, were victims of bombing in World War II; the **Auberge d'Allemagne** gave way to St Paul's Anglican Cathedral in 1839.

The final two existing *auberges* are both near the Anglican Cathedral. The **Auberge d'Aragon**, a simple single-storey building designed by Cassar on Independence Square, is the oldest *auberge*, dating from 1571. It now houses the Ministry for Justice and Home Affairs. The **Auberge de Bavière**, in the former Palace of Bali Carner (1696), looks straight out to sea and housed the Anglo-Bavarian *langue* throughout its existence from 1784–98.

Buildings of the Knights ★★★

The Knights' legacy to Malta includes many other outstanding buildings, chief among them the **Sacra Infirmeria**, or Holy Infirmary. The mighty hospital, high above Grand Harbour, was founded in 1574, soon after the Knights' relocation from Birgu, and was remarkably well equipped throughout the Knights' stay.

With the French occupation of Malta in 1800, the Sacra Infirmeria was looted of the silver plate that financed patient care and became a military hospital, a role it continued to play under the British until 1920. Casualties from the Gallipoli landings were brought here in 1915. Medical history was made in 1887 with the discovery of the brucellosis bacteria by David Bruce.

Four direct hits by World War II bombs reduced parts of the infirmary to rubble. Restoration work shelved through lack of funds in 1960 resumed in 1974 and the building reopened as the prestigious **Mediterranean Conference Centre** in 1979. The main Republic Hall and adjacent rooms were rebuilt in 1987 after a fire caused by a laser beam ignited the main stage curtain.

Above: *The splendid Auberge d'Italie now houses a ministry.*

KNIGHTS' HOSPITAL

The Great Ward of the **Sacra Infirmeria**, 155m (170yd) long and 10.5m (34ft) wide, was the world's longest hospital ward. It held 563 beds and could take 914 in times of emergency. Unusually for the time, each patient had a bed to himself with a woollen mattress. Meals for Knights and civilian patients were served on silver plate by the Knights themselves – even the Grand Master fulfilled his obligation to the Order by taking a turn of meal duty.

Cultural gatherings have taken place in the **Manoel Theatre** for far longer – since 1731, when Grand Master Manoel de Vilhena ordered that it be built 'for the honest recreation of the people', with funding from his own pocket. The little box theatre, in Old Theatre Street, is one of Europe's oldest and guided tours of the theatre and its museum are available.

In Merchants Street, opposite the Auberge d'Italie, is the 18th-century **Palazzo Parisio**, Napoleon's head-quarters from 12–18 June during the French occupation in 1798. It is now the Ministry of Foreign Affairs.

Streets and Squares ★★

The city's main artery is **Republic Street**, running the length of Valletta from the City Gate entrance to Fort St Elmo at its northern tip and traffic-free for much of its length. Here are the shops and cafés, crammed together in no sort of order, that give Valletta its social buzz.

In the morning, Republic Street throngs with laden shoppers, besuited businessmen and T-shirted tourists. In early afternoon it is much quieter – most shops close from 13:00 until 16:00, leaving the coffee bars and souvenir shops to do business. From late afternoon until the shut-ters come down at 19:00, the strip teems with life, though with less bustle now as this is strolling time for the young Maltese.

Below: *No cars here: a long street of steps in Malta's capital.*

Just inside City Gate is colonnaded **Freedom Square**, unfortunately used as a car park. Beyond it on the right is the bombed-out shell of the **Opera House** (*see* p. 45); its truncated columns and lower stonework are all that remains.

Follow Republic Street, with its tiny shops and boutiques shoulder to shoulder with the occasional church or ministry building, past the National Archaeological Museum in the Auberge de Provence on your left, to **Great Siege Square**, with the **Great Siege Monument** by Antonio Scibberas (1879–1947), which is situated opposite the huge bulk of the post-war, columned **Law Courts**. To the right, as you pass Zammit's colourful flower kiosk, **St John Square**, with its cafés and restaurants spilling outside in summer, sets off the mighty façade of St John's Co-Cathedral.

Republic Street leads on to **Republic Square**, filled with the bright umbrellas of alfresco cafés. It is a popular spot in summer. Across the street is the ornate **Caffe Cordina**, established in 1837 in the Knights' former treasury, which has a finely painted vaulted ceiling by Giuseppe Cali and unusual central bar.

In the square, Valenti's marble statue of **Queen Victoria** presides. At the back, above the arcade, the pleasing façade belongs to the **National Library**, or Bibliotheca. It was completed around 1796, just before the Knights' exit from Malta, and houses a highly valuable collection of books, documents and manuscripts dating back 800 years.

On display in glass-topped cabinets protected by green cloth are many records of the Knights, including the Processi Nobili documents that proved a Knight's nobility. Fortunately they survived Napoleon's order to have them destroyed during the French occupation.

There is a copy of the act by which Malta and Gozo passed from the hands of Charles V to the Knights and a letter of King Henry VIII, sent from Hampton Court on 22 November 1530, in which he congratulates Grand Master Philippe Villiers de l'Isle Adam on the Knights' acquisition of Malta. In another document, Henry VIII styles himself as Supreme Head of the Church of England and Protector of the Order. Also on show are the original plans of 1721 for the Manoel Theatre. To the right of the National Library is The Great Siege of Malta, described as Europe's most exciting 3D walk-through adventure.

Above: *Queen Victoria reigns in Republic Square.*

WHAT'S IN A NAME?

When Malta became a republic in 1974, it was time to change the names of many streets and squares in Valletta once again. So Kingsway (formerly Strada San Giorgio, Rue Nationale under the French and then Strada Reale) became Republic Street, Queen's Square turned into Republic Square, Kingsgate (formerly Porta Reale) was renamed City Gate, Kingsgate Arcade became Freedom Square and Britannia Street gave way to Melita Street. Much earlier, the British had rechristened Piazza San Giorgio as Palace Square, a name it retains today.

Immediately beyond, Valletta's main thoroughfare opens on to **Palace Square**, the true heart of Valletta, one side of which is occupied by the Palace of the Grand Masters. Much could be made of the area, which is sometimes used for car parking.

One block to your right is **Merchants Street**, with its family-run shops and businesses which have somehow survived down the years. An upstairs indoor food market offers exceptional fruit and vegetables among a variety of wares; one shop sells nothing but eggs. Another of Valletta's streets of note is **Strait Street**, but for a different historical reason. As the notorious 'Gut', it was packed with hostess bars and dance halls and was a favourite watering-hole of the Navy when the British ran Malta.

Above: *A small store in Valletta. Such family businesses are still common.*

TWIN-TOWER STYLE

The twin towers of **St John's Co-Cathedral**, a revolutionary architectural style for mid-16th century Malta that probably derived from Spain, set the pattern for church building in the Maltese islands. There are more than 350 churches and chapels throughout the Maltese islands. Many larger churches have a clock on each tower, one a working timepiece and the other painted on – in the firm belief that this would confuse the devil.

St John's Co-Cathedral ★★★

The façade is plain, even austere; inside it is sumptuous beyond belief. If Malta's treasures were listed, the Co-Cathedral would easily be at the head. As the former Conventual Church of the Knights, it was granted status as the Co-Cathedral, together with Mdina Cathedral, by Pope Pius VII in 1816.

The church is dedicated to John the Baptist, patron saint of the Order, and is regarded as the finest work of Maltese architect Gerolamo Cassar. The Knights' most important building was created between 1573 and 1577, a priority once Valletta's fortifications had been built and the streets laid down.

One of the two towers facing on to St John Square bears a clock with three faces which accurately tell the hour, day of the week and date in the month. Through the entrance below, the cathedral's barrel-vaulted interior and gilded walls create an overwhelming impression. The oil-painted ceiling, the masterpiece of Mattia Preti, depicts 18 episodes in the life of John the Baptist.

Left: *The plain façade of St John's Co-Cathedral hides a magnificent array of treasures within.*

Almost all of the Grand Masters who served in Malta are buried here. The French Grand Masters L'Isle Adam and La Valette are among 12 entombed in the crypt; others occupy strikingly ornate Baroque tombs in many of the 12 expensively gilded, sculpted and decorated chapels of the Knights' *langues* on either side of the nave. Others of Maltese nobility lie buried beneath the richly coloured marble slabs that cover the floor.

The silver gates to the last chapel on the right, the Chapel of the Blessed Sacrament, were painted black in 1798 to conceal their real value from the occupying French. The ploy worked and the gates, mistaken for iron, were left while other parts of the church were looted.

The Co-Cathedral's fine Flemish tapestries, based on works by Rubens and Poussin, are kept in the Cathedral Museum, accessed from Republic Street, and adorn the nave during the Festival of St John in mid-June.

Churches of Valletta ★★★

Valletta's churches are one of the city's outstanding features and some should not be missed out of a tour. **Our Lady of Victories**, Valletta's oldest building (1567), is in Victory Square by the bombed-out Opera House, on the site where Grand Master La Valette laid Valletta's foundation stone. It is attributed to Francesco Laparelli and Gerolamo Cassar and honours the Knights' triumph over the Turks in the Great Siege of 1565. It was given its Baroque appearance in the 17th century.

MALTA'S MASTERPIECE

Malta's best-known painting is *The Beheading of John the Baptist*, a masterpiece by the Italian painter **Michelangelo Merisi da Caravaggio** (1573–1610) and his only surviving signed work. It hangs in St John's Co-Cathedral museum; another of his paintings, *St Jerome*, is in the fourth chapel on the left. Both were commissioned by the French Grand Master **Alof de Wignacourt** during Caravaggio's 15-month stay in Malta from July 1607. Received into the Order on 14 July 1608, Caravaggio was imprisoned in Castel Sant' Angelo after a quarrel with a fellow Knight, but escaped by night and fled to neighbouring Sicily.

Above: *St Paul Shipwreck Church recalls the Apostle's arrival in Malta in AD 60.*

Another of Valletta's first churches, possibly also designed by Cassar, is the **St Paul Shipwreck Church**, commemorating St Paul's arrival in Malta in AD 60. The painted and gilded wooden figure of the apostle by prominent Maltese sculptor Melchiore Gafa which stands to the left of the altar is carried through Valletta each year on the saint's feast day, 10 February. The church contains one of St Paul's arm bones and a section of the column on which he was beheaded; it also possesses a prized silver collection.

Also dedicated to St Paul is the neo-classical **St Paul's Pro Cathedral**, the former Anglican Cathedral, with its huge, 65m (210ft) spire shaping Valletta's skyline. It was built in 1844 and funded by the Dowager Queen Adelaide, distressed on her visit in 1839 that there was no Anglican church in Valletta. Its site in Independence Square was formerly that of the small Auberge d'Allemagne, built in 1574 and knocked down to make way for the cathedral.

Cassar built most of the Knights' churches in Valletta – such as the original **Carmelite Church**, which was replaced in 1958 after its destruction in World War II by the much larger domed edifice that now rivals the St Paul's Pro Cathedral. Others of Cassar's churches were eventually rebuilt and include **St Augustine**, shaped as a Greek cross and modified in Baroque style, and **St Catherine of Italy** (1713), the domed church of the Italian *langue* opposite Our Lady of Victories.

The **Church of Gesu** remains the University of Malta church, although the main body of students was relocated to new premises at Tal Qroqq, above Msida, over a quarter of a century ago. It is part of the university building which was formerly the Jesuit College of Studies. In Republic Street near City Gate is the **Church of St Barbara**, where Catholic services are held in English, French and German.

THE CAPITAL'S MUSEUMS

The museums of Malta are fittingly housed in a selection of the country's finest old buildings. As well as viewing the exhibits, visitors can gaze upon 16th-century interiors or, in the case of the National War Museum, enjoy a close look at Fort St Elmo.

National Museum of Archaeology ★★★

Situated in the Auberge de Provence on Republic Street, the museum contains a priceless collection of artefacts saved from prehistoric temple and tomb sites throughout the Maltese islands. It does a fine presentation job on ancient pottery, sculpted temple stones, figurines, weapons and jewellery – they are particularly interesting if you have visited or intend visiting the temple sites.

Of particular note are the sculpted Copper Age blocks from Tarxien with their spiral motifs – these are the originals; those at the temple site are copies. Water-colours show the temples as they would have appeared and there are detailed models of the prehistoric sites.

National Museum of Fine Arts ★★

Recognized for its impressive assembly of both Maltese and foreign paintings from the 14th century to the present day, this collection includes work by Mattia Preti, whose Maltese masterpiece was the ceiling of St John's Co-Cathedral, the 18th-century artist Antoine de Favray and 17th-century painter Guido Reni.

The museum, in South Street, is housed in one of Valletta's earliest palaces, dating from 1571 and rebuilt in the 1760s. From 1821 it was the residence of the Royal Navy's commander in chief and known as Admiralty House; among its famous occupants was Lord Mountbatten of Burma, in World War II the commander of the British Mediterranean fleet.

MUSEUM HOURS

The opening times of the Heritage Malta museums are 09:00–17:00 daily including Sunday, with last admission time 16:30. Museums are closed on 24, 25 and 31 December, 1 January and Good Friday. Admission fees vary; there are special rates for students aged 12–17 and over 60s. Under 5s can visit free. There are multisite tickets for Xaghra (Gozo), Victoria Citadel (Gozo), Malta temples and Rabat/Mdina. The State Rooms in the Palace of the Grand Masters are open daily except Thursday 10:00–16:00. The Hal Saflieni Hypogeum (see p. 72) only allows 80 visitors per day – book online at www.heritagemaltashop.com

Below: *Malta's Siege Bell commemorates the dead of World War II.*

SIEGE BELL OF MALTA

Since May 1992, the 50th
anniversary of the George
Cross award to the islands,
the 8000 British and Maltese
who perished in the second
Siege of Malta from 1940–43
have been commemorated
by the 10-tonne bronze
Siege Bell which is found
beneath its cupola high
above Grand Harbour near
the Lower Barracca Gardens.
The work of English sculptor
Michael Sanders, it was
unveiled during a visit by
Queen Elizabeth II and is
rung on 15 August each year
to mark the lifting of the
World War II siege by the
Santa Maria convoy.

Below: *St Barbara Bastion
and Barriera Wharf, part of
the imposing fortifications
along Valletta's Grand
Harbour shore.*

National War Museum ★★★

Appropriately located in Fort St Elmo, the museum re-
kindles awareness of the battle for Malta in World War
II. Exhibits include the restored Gloster Gladiator biplane
Faith, General Eisenhower's jeep *Husky*, sections of
wrecked aircraft, torpedoes and anti-tank guns. Pictures
indicate the extent of Malta's wartime suffering.

The Fortifications ★★

Arriving in Malta by sea, the first landmark you pass
entering Grand Harbour is star-shaped **Fort St Elmo** on
the exposed tip of the Valletta peninsula. Under massive
bombardment, it defied the Turks for 31 days in the Great
Siege of 1565. The fort was rebuilt in 1567 and has since
been strengthened and enlarged by the Knights and the
British; it now houses the National War Museum.

Leading out to Fort St Elmo on both sides of the tiny
peninsula are the mighty **curtain walls** behind which
Valletta took shape. On the landward side, now separating
Valletta from its suburb of Floriana, the defences are
strengthened by four mighty **bastions** and are further
protected by a wide moat 18m (60ft) deep.

The City Gate entrance cuts through the curtain wall
between **St John's Cavalier** and **St James Cavalier**; in all,
11 bastions ring the city. Sections of wall are still known
by the *langues* which protected them – French, English
and German Curtain. All around the peninsula there are
stunning views out to sea or
across the two great har-
bours; below **St Salvatore
Bastion** on the Marsamxett
side is the **Manderaggio**,
a sheltered inlet used by the
Knights.

The Barracca Gardens ★★

Two minutes' walk from
the Auberge de Castile et
Leon are the arcaded **Upper
Barracca Gardens**, a 17th-

century parade ground of the Italian Knights with spectacular cross-harbour views. Among the trees and shrubs are a charming replica sculpture of three children, titled *Les Gavroches,* by Antonio Sciortino, a bronze bust of British prime minister Sir Winston Churchill and a collection of monuments. There is also the tomb of Sir Thomas Maitland, British Governor from 1813–24. The Noonday Gun is fired from the Saluting Battery below the gardens at midday.

Above: *The Upper Barracca Gardens by Grand Harbour.*

The **Lower Barracca Gardens**, at the bottom end of St Christopher Street, enclose a small Grecian temple monument with a statue of Sir Alexander Ball, civil commissioner when the British took over the islands in 1800. To the left when you enter Valletta through City Gate is **Hastings Garden**, named after the Marquis of Hastings, Governor of Malta from 1824–26.

Casa Rocca Piccola ★★

This nobleman's house, a short way past the Palace of the Grand Masters at 74 Republic Street, provides an excellent insight into domestic life in the upper echelons of Maltese society from the late 17th century. It was one of Valletta's early buildings, erected for the Knights' Italian *langue* around 1580, and over the years became home to many top-ranking Knights and a bishop before being sold into Maltese nobility in 1784. It survived the war undamaged.

Today, Casa Rocca Piccola is the Valletta home of the De Piro family; the parents of Nicholas, present Marquis de Piro and Baroncino of Budaq, have an apartment there. It is the only historic Valletta house open to the public and a guided tour takes in the tiny upstairs chapel, bedroom, drawing room, library, sitting room and dining room; also a costume collection.

THE OPERA HOUSE

The bomb-devastated remains of Valletta's Opera House remain a legacy of World War II. The building, designed by **Edward Barry** of Covent Garden fame, was completed in 1866 and immediately took over from the small Manoel Theatre as the capital's leading place of entertainment. Since its destruction in 1942, redevelopment of the site, now used as a car park, has been much discussed – whether to rebuild in the original style or start afresh. Climb the steps off Republic Street to gain an impression of its former grandeur.

FLOATING TAXIS

The traditional way to cross Grand Harbour is by *dgħajsa* (pronounced 'dicer') – Malta's answer to the gondola – the high-prowed, brightly painted water taxi that once ferried Royal Navy sailors back to their ships. Traditionally propelled by a standing oarsman, they now have outboard motors. Many boats are based along Senglea's and Vittoriosa's waterfront, so it may be easier to start a round-trip on the Three Cities side. Annual *dgħajsa* races are held in Grand Harbour on 8 September.

Lascaris War Rooms ★★

Deep inside Lascaris Bastion, the Malta Command Centre – better known as the Lascaris War Rooms and nerve centre of Allied operations in the Mediterranean during World War II – is an ever-present reminder of Malta's vital role in the defeat of the Axis forces. Within the network of rooms, the war effort was directed by such eminent wartime leaders as Generals **Montgomery**, **Alexander** and **Eisenhower**, Admiral **Cunningham** and Air Marshall **Tedder**.

Here the critical decisions were taken which saved Malta from Axis clutches and set up the Allies' Alamein success. It is presented as a live museum, with 60 or so life-size figures at work in the wireless rooms, cipher room, guns operation room, RAF room and other chambers; each scene is frozen from a particular phase of the war. A personal headphone guide is available and most of the displays are accessible to disabled visitors.

More Museums ★★

Valletta's museums are not confined to art and ancient artefacts. The Museum Egalite in South Street is the general Workers' Union's own museum, taking visitors through six decades of the GWU in Malta. The Toy Museum, at 222 Republic Street, is aimed at children, but will appeal to their parents, too – three floors of exhibits include Dinky, Corgi and Matchbox cars.

Below: *Grand Harbour is a port of call on a growing number of Mediterranean cruising programmes.*

GRAND HARBOUR ★★★

Arguably the world's greatest natural deepwater harbour, Grand Harbour penetrates inland for nearly 3.5km (2¼ miles) from **St Elmo Point** and **Ricasoli Point** at its entrance to the dockyards of **Marsa Creek**. Focal point of Malta's two great sieges, when it sheltered vast naval fleets, Grand Harbour today sees only limited commercial activity and cruise ships. The cruise traffic is steadily being developed following the building of the cruise terminal below Lascaris Bastion.

From Valletta you can identify (from the left) **Kalkara Creek**, **Dockyard Creek** and **French Creek** below the Three Cities promontories of Vittoriosa and Senglea (*see* p. 59). The **Dockyard**, which employed more than 13,000 men – 15% of Malta's workforce – before Britain's naval withdrawal, now provides work for fewer than 5000, mostly in the ship repair yards.

Grand Harbour is best explored on the 75-minute **Harbour Cruise** that departs several times daily from the Strand at Sliema and also takes in **Marsamxett Harbour** and the creeks of the Three Cities.

Old Customs House ★

On Lascaris Wharf, near the remains of a lift that once descended from Upper Barracca Gardens, is the elegant Venetian-styled Customs House of Giuseppe Bonici, dating from 1774. The building is not open to the public.

FLORIANA

Floriana, a Valletta suburb of ministries, gardens and open spaces inside its own commanding fortifications, has its origins in the 1630s, when it was decided to strengthen Valletta's landward defences against further Turkish attacks. It takes its name from Paolo Floriani, an Italian military engineer dispatched by Pope Urban VIII.

Beyond the land-side curtain wall, with its deep defensive ditch, a second bastioned fortification rises from Pieta Creek and crosses the peninsula to Grand Harbour. The high wall extends along both coasts and is spectacularly floodlit at night. Impressive as the fortifications are, however, they were never

> ### THE GRANARIES
>
> The flat, circular stone slabs dotted about **St Publius Square** in front of Floriana's parish church cover the granaries, vast subterranean pits that served as the grain stores of the Knights. There are similar granaries near the main entrance to **Fort St Elmo**. Grain had to be imported from the Knights' estates in Europe, Sicily and Tunisia to offset deficiencies in the local crop.

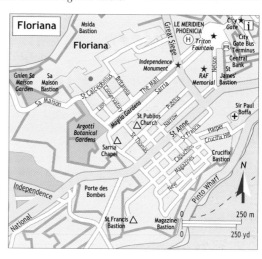

PORTE DES BOMBES

The way into and out of Floriana is through, or around, the imposing Porte des Bombes, a ceremonial twin-arched gateway at the limit of the fortifications now isolated from the curtain wall by carriageways of the main access road. The first of the two archways was built under Grand Master **Ramon Perellos** in the early 1700s to celebrate military success against the Turks; the second archway was added in the same style in 1868.

Below: *The Porte des Bombes gateway into Floriana. Along with many of the suburb's fortifications, it is attractively floodlit at night.*

tested by armed attack. Work began on the streets and buildings of Floriana nearly a century later, in 1722.

Prominent in The Mall, by the Valletta bus terminus from which routes radiate out to every town and village in the island, is the five-star **Le Meridien Phoenicia**, the grand old lady of Malta's hotels.

Churches and Gardens ★★

Beyond the Phoenicia Hotel and the Independence monument of 1964 are the tree-lined **Maglio Gardens**, once an exercise ground of the Knights, with statues of Maltese worthies. Further on are the **Argotti Botanical Gardens**, created in 1774 and packed with unusual specimens from all over the world. Below the Argotti Gardens are gardens dedicated to the Catholic saint Philip Neri and a plant nursery. The open space by the Maglio Gardens is **Independence Arena**, once a military parade area and now a sports ground.

The gardens lead past **St Publius Church**, built between 1733 and 1768 and named after the Roman governor whom St Paul converted to Christianity in AD 60. The church, which faces Valletta, was the last parish church built by the Knights. The work of Giuseppe Bonici, it was twice partly rebuilt; further reconstruction took place after World War II. Nearby on a street corner is the round **Sarria Chapel**, built in 1678 to designs by Lorenzo Gafa and containing seven paintings by Mattia Preti.

So close to Valletta, Floriana has had no need to develop as a shopping centre. Small bars and grocery stores serve the town houses either side of arcaded St Anne Street, the main route towards Valletta from the rest of the island. Among the web of tightly knit streets are the Malta police headquarters and a number of government buildings, among them the offices of the Inland Revenue.

Valletta at a Glance

Valletta is best explored out of the peak holiday months of Jul and Aug, when there are fewer tourists in town and it is not quite so hot. Malta's capital is busy all year and especially on the feast day of St Paul, 10 Feb.

Buses operate at frequent intervals from all parts of the island to the Valletta terminus at City Gate – they run half-hourly from the airport to Valletta. Those arriving by **car** should use the multi-storey car park outside City Gate, as Valletta's streets are narrow and parking is extremely limited. A half-hourly passenger-only **ferry** service operates from Sliema – the five-minute cross-harbour journey is far quicker than by road.

Everyone **walks** as driving is virtually impossible around Valletta – most streets are narrow and some, like the main shopping strip of Republic Street, are for pedestrians only. If you insist on having a set of wheels, take a horse-drawn *karrozzin* ride around the city.

Maltese hotels are graded from five stars downwards; the grading reflects both facilities and price.
Le Meridien Phoenicia, The Mall, Floriana, tel: 2122

5241, fax: 2123 5254. Grand old lady of Malta's hotels, built in 1947. Real five-star sophistication by City Gate.
Osborne, 50 South Street, tel: 2124 3656/7, fax: 2124 7293. Classy three-star in a quiet area of Valletta.
Castille, Castille Square, tel: 2124 3678, fax: 2124 3679. Central position near Upper Barracca Gardens for this modest three-star with its own wine bar.
Grand Harbour, Battery Street, tel: 2124 6003, fax: 2124 2219. Two-star hotel with fine views over Grand Harbour.

Malata, Palace Square, tel: 2123 3967. French-Mediterranean, with speciality dishes changed daily. Good lunchtime blackboard menu.
The Carriage, South Street, tel: 2124 7828. Traditional restaurant, open lunchtimes and weekend evenings.
D'Agostino, Republic Street, tel: 2122 5197. Italian-based with wide menu; near the Palace of the Grand Masters.
Giannini, Windmill Street, tel: 2123 7121. Daily specialities support more expensive Italian-style menu.
The Lantern, Sappers Street, tel: 2123 7521. Family-run restaurant specializing in traditional Maltese fare.
Sicilia, St John Street, tel: 2157 2984. Inexpensive, top-quality lunchtime fish and pasta terrace overlooking Grand Harbour.

Trattoria Palazz, Old Theatre Street, tel: 2122 6611. Cellar restaurant with inviting menu off Republic Square.
La Cave, Castille Square, tel: 2124 3678. Pizzas, pasta and choice of 100-plus wines in a 400-year-old cellar.
Caffe Cordina, Republic street, tel: 2123 4385. Traditional coffee house with vaulted, frescoed ceiling.

Many local tour companies offer excursions from the main resort areas to Valletta. A typical tour of the capital takes in the Upper Barracca Gardens, St John's Co-Cathedral, the National War Museum, Lascaris War Rooms and Palace of the Grand Masters. Sunday morning tours visit the market. Times and departure points vary from company to company. Two operators with extensive tour programmes are Josephine's, 80 The Strand, Sliema, tel: 2131 0435; and Nova Tours, Bay Square, Buġibba, tel: 2157 5240, 2157 5960.

Tourist information, 1 City Gate, Valletta, tel: 2123 7747.
Police, tel: 191 (general inquiries 2122 4001).
St Luke's Hospital, tel: 2124 1251.
Airport (flight inquiries), tel: 2124 9600.
Taxi (24-hour service), tel: 2131 3261.

3
Sliema and
St Julian's

If size alone determined a country's capital, then Sliema would win hands down. This pleasant seaside resort, much changed over the years, is by far Malta's largest town. It is at the centre of a coastal sprawl reaching from **Pieta**, at the foot of Floriana's towering curtain walls, westwards to **St George's Bay** and embracing **Ta' Xbiex**, **Gzira**, **Balluta**, **Spinola** and **Paceville**.

This is the focus of Malta's thriving tourism industry, thickly spread with hotels, restaurants and bars and catering to the needs of a good proportion of Malta's 1.2 million annual visitors. While Valletta remains the history-laden capital, it is Sliema and St Julian's that present the modern face of Malta.

SLIEMA

Sliema's most notable feature is its **seafront**, stretching for 8km (5 miles) from Pieta to St Julian's past the Marsamxett yacht marinas of Msida Creek and Lazzaretto Creek, Tigne headland and the smooth rocky foreshore lining the Mediterranean. However, the one-time elegance of **Tower Road** running towards Balluta Bay has been lost forever through haphazard planning.

High-rise, glass-fronted apartment blocks have replaced all but a handful of the brightly shuttered stone town houses that once lined this stretch, dominated since the 1960s by the Preluna Hotel, a 14-storey intrusion on Sliema's skyline which until a few years ago had the doubtful honour of being Malta's tallest building.

MEDITERRANEAN SEA
Żebbuġ · Gozo
· Victoria
Mġarr · Comino
Mellieħa · · Buġibba · St Julian's
Għajn Tuffieħa · VALLETTA · Sliema
Malta Rabat · Hamrun · · Żabbar
· Luqa
Birżebbuġa ·
MEDITERRANEAN SEA

DON'T MISS

*** **Harbour cruise from Sliema:** the best excursion of the Maltese islands.
*** **Spinola Bay:** one of the most picturesque locations on the island.
** **St George's Bay:** centre of Malta's nightlife with its new sandy beach.

Opposite: *Msida's creekside parish church of St Joseph all dressed up for the summer* festa.

THE HARBOUR CRUISE

Malta's excursion *par excellence* is the harbour cruise that operates several times daily from the Strand at Sliema. The trip, with commentary, is a history lesson in itself. It lasts around an hour and a quarter and takes in every creek in Grand Harbour and Marsamxett Harbour. Other pleasure boats leave here for a day trip to Comino and an excursion around the Maltese islands; there are also day excursions on a wide range of other craft.

The early character of Sliema was shaped in the first years of the century, when the town became recognized as the most fashionable part of the country in which to live. Today, the apartments piled high along Tower Road are the most expensive in Malta. Behind the twisting coast road, it is quite easy to become lost in the maze of densely populated back streets of old Sliema. You will eventually land up at the water's edge again – but most probably not where you expected to be.

The resort's traditional centre is still known as the **Ferries**. From here, steamers once crossed the harbour to Valletta; the service was revived a few years ago and a half-hourly service operates year-round between the capital and Sliema. Pleasure cruises also start from here.

Manoel Island ★

The dual carriageway that hugs the shoreline sweeps away from Sliema's pavement cafés to pass the narrow bridge leading on to Manoel Island, now a renowned yachting centre and home to the 160-year-old Royal Malta Yacht Club (like the golf club, it has retained its 'royal' identity from colonial times). Successive plans to turn Manoel Island into a fully fledged tourist centre, with five-star hotels and other amenities, have yet to reach fruition.

Below: *The tightly packed buildings, old and new, along Sliema's waterfront.*

At the far end of the island, **Fort Manoel**, now in poor condition, was built between 1723 and 1732 for Grand Master Manoel de Vilhena and could accommodate 500 men. The French garrison were held here in 1800 before being sent home.

The Knights built an isolation hospital for infectious diseases in the early 17th century; the elegant, arcaded **Lazaretto of San Rocco** building, which subsequently cared for World War I casualties, still looks out on the old quarantine anchorage.

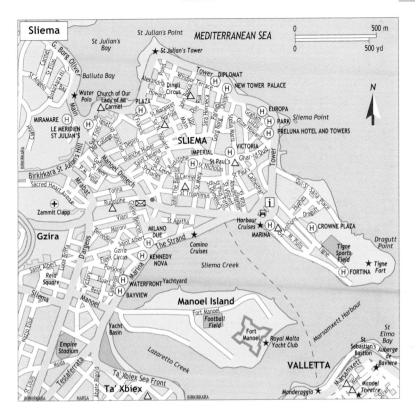

Gzira ★

On the landward side is residential Gzira, whose rusting sports stadium just off the seafront once staged Malta's international soccer matches. All important games, including the entire Premier Division programme in the national soccer league, are now staged at the modern Ta' Qali stadium in the centre of the island.

Gzira runs into **Ta' Xbiex**, with a flotilla of ocean-going and smaller craft occupying the berths of Ta' Xbiex and Msida marinas; foreign embassies occupy prime seafront positions and bougainvillea-adorned villas are tucked away among tree-lined side roads. At the entrance to Msida Creek, high and dry on the foreshore,

Below: *Spinola Bay at St Julian's, a popular spot for restaurants, still exudes a fishing village atmosphere.*

is the brigantine **Black Pearl**, which featured in the 1980 film *Popeye* (*see* p. 101) and is now a restaurant.

At the end of the creek, opposite the well-planted gardens bordering Marina Street, is the dominant **St Joseph's**, parish church of **Msida**, built in 1893. However, if the smooth-rock, Mediterranean foreshore has more appeal – the promenade walk from Sliema to St Julian's is always a delight, but watch out for speeding rollerbladers – head inland up the hill from the Ferries, shortly to emerge on the seaward coast. You have cut across the neck of the Tigne peninsula, at the end of which, facing Valletta, is **Tigne Fort**, built on Dragutt Point in 1761 by Grand Master Manuel Pinto de Fonseca to provide cross-harbour cover for Fort St Elmo.

ST JULIAN'S ★★★

While Sliema fills more holiday brochure pages than any other part of Malta, it is to St Julian's, its neighbour Paceville and St George's Bay that Malta's young people flock each Friday and Saturday night. The two areas have a completely different approach to what passes as nightlife; while Sliema has retained something of its sedate past, along the coast there is an unbridled brashness in the disco bars, clubs and fast-food outlets that have mushroomed since the 1990s.

However, the former fishing village at the head of Spinola Bay clings on to its old charm. In summer, St Julian's presents a colourful scene. Brightly painted *luzzu* boats bob in the bay and fishing folk still go about their business – the men unravelling and drying their nets; the women selling the day's catch.

Some of Malta's best restaurants are here, making use of the pair of fine old arched boathouses that once stood like twin sentinels in the grounds of majestic **Spinola Palace**. The palace, built in 1688 by Paolo Rafael Spinola, Grand Prior of Lombardy, is an architectural masterpiece that itself contains a restaurant. A promenade extends the length of the bay towards the newly rebuilt Cavalieri Hotel.

Spinola Bay is but a narrow extension of wider St Julian's Bay; across the bay, on Tower Road leading from Sliema, is **St Julian's Tower**, one of several coastal fortifications erected at the time of Grand Master Martin de Redin in the late 1650s. Situated between Sliema and St Julian's is tiny **Balluta Bay**, with its mini-promenade of palm trees, and swish new five-star Le Meridien St Julian's Hotel. Balluta's main seafront features are the Church of Our Lady of Mount Carmel and the water polo pools opposite.

Paceville ★★

Beyond St Julian's, narrow St George's Road climbs from the bay towards Paceville – a stretch of road invariably thronged with holiday-makers and heavy with traffic. Away to the right, the unappealing 22-storey tower dominating this stretch of coastline is the business centre of Portomaso, a development that includes the 220-room Hilton Hotel, luxury apartments, restaurants and a

> ### HORSE-DRAWN CABS
>
> If the promenade walk from Sliema to St Julian's looks too taxing under the powerful sun, hail a *karrozzin*, Malta's traditional horse-drawn carriage, and travel there in style. There are *karrozzini* ranks at Sliema, St Julian's, Valletta and outside the gateway to Mdina.

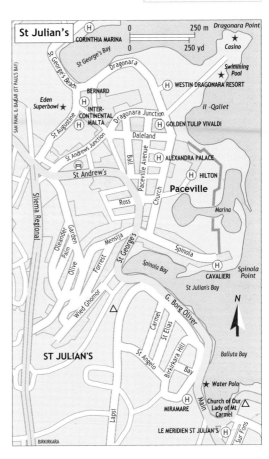

Above: *Water's-edge sunbathing lido and pool of the Fortina Hotel, Sliema.*

yacht marina. The modern Hilton has replaced its stylish namesake of the 1960s; on an adjacent site, the grand 300-room Westin Dragonara Resort has taken the place of the former Dragonara Palace, another 1960s hotel, giving the area a distinctly upmarket feel.

Paceville's half-dozen narrow streets are a mix of traditional town houses, hotels, bars and restaurants – fewer of the former and more of the latter as this compact area has turned itself over almost entirely to catering for tourists. The range of restaurants is extensive, from Scandinavian to Italian, American to Chinese. Out of all proportion to the area is the massive St George's Park apartment complex, Malta's largest.

FESTA COLOUR

Adorning the façade of the parish church with hundreds of coloured lightbulbs is the first stage of every village's elaborate *festa* preparations. The result is stunning – nowhere more than at **Msida**, where the lights on the parish church of St Joseph reflect vividly in Msida Creek. Then come the decorations – the statues of saints lining every street, the bunting draped from house to house, the flags atop every other building and yet more fairy lights strung between poles. Finally come the car decorations – for the day after the *festa*, when everyone heads off in convoy for a picnic on the beach.

St George's Bay ★★

Development is continuing rapidly past Paceville's neon city and around tiny St George's Bay, redevelopment of which was completed in summer 2005 with the creation of a beach with sand imported from Jordan. The bay sports two hotels of Corinthia Hotels International – the five-star Corinthia San Gorg, built around a coastal defensive tower, and Corinthia Marina. Around the point is another five-star hotel, the Radisson SAS Bay Point Resort, and just inland of the beach the Inter-Continental Malta opposite the modern Baystreet shopping complex.

Both Paceville and St George's Bay were quiet and commercially undeveloped two decades ago. Now they have magnetic appeal for Malta's youth, who arrive in droves for their weekend infusion of disco decibels at a score of neon-lit clubs and bars such as Empire and The Edge. A tenpin bowling centre and 16-screen cinema complex are further attractions.

Sliema and St Julian's at a Glance

The resorts are at their best outside the peak season, as during July and August holiday crowds throng the pavements and finding a restaurant table can be a problem.

There is parking for your **car** on the long seafront road or in Sliema's maze of back streets. A half-hourly **ferry** service operates from Valletta year-round. **Buses** operate half-hourly from the airport to Valletta – change at the City Gate terminus for Sliema.

Buses run along the seafront on either side of Sliema; alternatively, pick up a horse-drawn *karrozzin*.

Sliema
Preluna Hotel & Spa, Tower Road, tel: 2133 4001/9; fax: 2134 2292. Four stars; high-rise seafront hotel.
Fortina, Tigne Seafront, tel: 2346 0000, fax: 2346 2162. All-inclusive with luxury spa.
Park, Graham Street, tel: 2134 3780, fax: 2134 3315. Four-star near the Preluna.
Bayview, The Strand, tel: 2132 0216, fax: 2134 6212. Well-priced three-star overlooking harbour.
Marina, Tigne Seafront, tel: 2133 6461, fax: 2133 0650. Traditional three-star.
Howard Johnson Diplomat,

Tower Road, tel: 2134 5361, fax: 2134 5351. Four-star hotel on the seafront road.

St Julian's/Paceville
Westin Dragonara Resort, tel: 2138 1000, fax: 2138 1347. This is an elegant five-star that's better than most.
Golden Tulip Vivaldi, Dragonara Road, tel: 2137 8100, fax: 2137 8101. Four-star in the heart of the nightlife area.

St George's Bay
InterContinental Malta, tel: 2137 7600, fax: 2137 2222. Outstanding five-star close to the beach and nightlife.
Corinthia San Gorg, tel: 2137 4114, fax: 2137 4039. Offering five-star luxury by the sea.
Radisson SAS Bay Point Resort, tel: 2137 4894, fax: 2137 4895. Five-star by the sea.

Sliema
Il Galeone, Tigne Seafront, tel: 2131 6420. Good Italian restaurant with a range of house specialities.
Lanca At Village Gossip, Tigne Seafront, tel: 2133 8743. Quality dining in a former hairdresser's, Village Gossip.
Blondino, Ghar il-Lembi Street, tel: 2134 4605. Inexpensive and appetizing seafood.

St Julian's
L-Ghonnella, tel: 2135 1027. Top-quality dining on the terrace of the 17th-century Spinola Palace.

La Dolce Vita, Spinola Bay, tel: 2133 7036. Lively restaurant with good fish menu and terrace.
Barracuda, Main Street, tel: 2133 1817. Higher-priced, quality water's-edge dining in a former summer residence dating from 1793.
Raffael, Spinola Bay, tel: 2135 2000. Excellent spot for pasta.
San Giuliano, Spinola Bay, tel: 2133 2000. Popular Italian in a former boathouse.
Fayrouz, Borg Olivier Street, tel: 2132 0837. Intimate Middle Eastern restaurant.

Paceville
Gino's, Ball Street, tel: 2135 1774. Excellent Maltese specialities, children half-price.
Ir-Rokna, Church Street, tel: 2138 4060. One of Malta's oldest restaurants/pizzerias.

Boat trips operate from the Strand at Sliema, Captain Morgan Cruises, tel: 2346 3333.
Island Tours are bookable at Josephine's, 80 The Strand, Sliema, tel: 2131 0435.
Dive specialists offering tuition from beginner to advanced level include: Diveshack, tel: 2133 8558; Dive Systems, tel: 2131 9123; Divewise Services, tel: 2135 6441.

Tourist information, 1 City Gate, Valletta, tel: 2123 7747.

4
The Three Cities

Look across Grand Harbour from Valletta's ramparts and spread before you is the panorama comprising **Vittoriosa**, **Cospicua** and **Senglea**, known collectively as the Three Cities. Although they are but small towns, they are historically important yet sadly tend to be overlooked by visitors to the Maltese islands.

There are no hotels or restaurants in the area, but this lack of tourist trappings is offset on the finger-shaped peninsulas of Vittoriosa and Senglea by some fine old buildings that pre-date Gerolamo Cassar's worthy edifices in Valletta. It was around these creeks that the Knights of the Order of St John established their first base on Malta in 1530 following their eviction from Rhodes.

New buildings that went up to accommodate the Knights included *auberges* for each of the *langues* and a hospital. New defences afforded some security on the landward side, but Birgu – now Vittoriosa – soon outgrew itself and by the 1560s had overspilled beyond the city walls to create a small suburb. This was called Bormla – now Cospicua (the conspicuous) – linking the other two around Dockyard Creek.

Meanwhile, on the peninsula adjacent to Birgu, the third of the Three Cities was developing as a town in its own right. Senglea, once called L'Isla but renamed after French Grand Master Claude de la Sengle on the completion of Fort St Michael in 1552 was, like its neighbours, destined to play a major role in the Great Siege of 1565.

DON'T MISS

*** Fort St Angelo:
the Three Cities' defensive masterpiece; former HQ of the Knights.
** Inquisitor's Palace:
see the courtroom, prison cells and torture chamber.
** Maritime Museum:
for a fascinating insight into Malta's seafaring past.
** Views of Grand Harbour:
from Senglea's Gardjola Garden.
** Cotonera Lines: dramatic fortification protecting the Three Cities.

Opposite: *Vedette watchtower at Senglea.*

THE KNIGHTS' DILEMMA

Arriving in Malta, the Knights faced two options – to settle inland at **Mdina** or by Grand Harbour in **Birgu**. Neither place met their needs, with Mdina too far inland and Birgu, while better sited, lacking fortifications. The Knights none too enthusiastically chose Birgu, a small town behind **Castello a Mare** (now Fort St Angelo) because it offered shelter for their galleys. It is now called Vittoriosa.

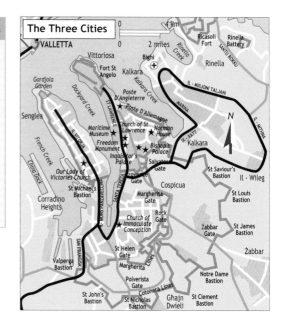

The Three Cities

Below: *Fort St Angelo was the Knights' headquarters in the Great Siege. It commands the entrance to Grand Harbour.*

Birgu was renamed Vittoriosa to commemorate the Great Siege victory (it is still known locally and often signposted as Birgu), but all three cities suffered badly in the mighty conflict with the Turks and when Valletta's foundation stone was laid in 1566, Birgu's days of influence over Maltese affairs were numbered. On 18 March 1571, the Knights crossed Grand Harbour amid great ceremony and moved into their new capital on Mount Sceberras.

With the development of Malta's shipbuilding industry, the Three Cities embraced a new identity as suburbs of Valletta, largely populated by dockyard workers. In World War II, they suffered severe damage from Axis bombers targeting Grand Harbour and the dockyards; Senglea and Cospicua were particularly badly hit.

VITTORIOSA
Fort St Angelo ★★★

This imposing fortress thrusting out into Grand Harbour at the tip of the Vittoriosa peninsula is an architectural masterpiece; restoration is currently in hand and part of the fort will eventually be turned into a museum that will be open to visitors. The fort was built by Grand Master **L'Isle Adam** soon after the Knights' arrival in 1530 on the site believed to have been occupied by Phoenician and Roman temples. Work involved strengthening an old **Arab** fortification on the site and embracing a mansion of the **De Nava family** and tiny **St Anne's Chapel**, both of which survive.

It became the Knights' headquarters and their command centre during the Great Siege of 1565, when it came under fierce bombardment after the fall of Fort St Elmo across Grand Harbour; its mighty cannon were capable of repelling any seaborne invasion by the Turks. Though restored in the late 17th century, the fort fell into disrepair. Some 350 years after the Knights had made Fort St Angelo their base, it again became a headquarters – this time of the **British Navy**, first as HMS Egmont and from 1933 as HMS St Angelo. In World War II, it suffered some 70 direct hits by bombs. In the mid-1980s it served briefly as a tourist complex.

Inquisitor's Palace ★★

The Office of the Inquisition existed to defend the Catholic faith and counter heresy. As the Pope's agent, the Inquisitor was stylishly housed in a Palace built around 1574. The increasingly ruthless holders of the office were ever unpopular with the Knights and Maltese alike through their abuse of power, yet two eventually became Pope and over twenty more became cardinals.

THE GREAT CHAIN

After Fort St Elmo had capitulated to the Turks during the Great Siege of 1565, the invaders turned their attentions across Grand Harbour to the peninsulas of Birgu (Vittoriosa) and L'Isla (Senglea). But the Knights had in place a defence with a difference – a huge chain, forged in Venice, that was strung across the entrance to Dockyard Creek between Fort St Angelo and Senglea. Evidence of the chain may still be seen below Fort St Angelo.

Below: *Carriage of the Inquisitor displayed in the Inquisitor's Palace.*

FREEDOM MONUMENT

On a rocky outcrop before the Church of St Lawrence, the Freedom Monument marks the British naval withdrawal from Malta in 1979. A bugler sounds off as the Maltese flag is raised; the handshake between Maltese worker and British sailor the amicable separation. The ceremony on Vittoriosa's waterfront marked the spot where Nelson's representative General Graham had landed in 1799, initiating 180 years of British military presence.

The palace, built around three courtyards, contains some grand rooms with wooden ceilings. The upper walls of the main hall bear all 62 Inquisitors' coats of arms – though unfilled after 1798, when the Office of the Inquisition was abolished under the French. Visitors can see the graffiti-adorned cells in which prisoners were held awaiting trial and also the execution yard.

Maritime Museum ★★

Malta's remarkable seafaring heritage long called out for such a museum. The building, the Royal Naval bakery, was designed by naval architect **William Scamp** in 1842 and has a distinctive clock tower styled on one in the British naval yard at Devonport. Vacated by the Navy in 1979, it became a museum in 1992 and includes sections highlighting the Knights, Royal Navy and merchant navy. The adjacent Casino di Venezia fronts the new marina.

The *Auberges* ★★

The Knights' *auberges* in Vittoriosa date from the 1530s, before the Order transferred to Valletta. Seven were built, of which four survive – the **Auberge de France**, **Auberge d'Auvergne et Provence**, **Auberge de Castile et Portugal** in Hilda Tabone Street and the **Auberge d'Angleterre** on adjoining Mistral Street.

The Auberge de France is the oldest and most impressive, built like the others in the style of Rhodes, to where the Knights probably hoped to return. The Auberge d'Angleterre now houses Vittoriosa library. Just off the main square in St Scholastica Street is the Knights' first **hospital**, built upon their arrival from Rhodes in 1530. The stern-fronted building was later used as a nunnery.

Church of St Lawrence ★★

This grand building facing across Dockyard Creek to Senglea is a 1691 reconstruction by Maltese architect **Lorenzo Gafa** of the former 16th-century Knights' Conventual Church. In view of its exposed waterfront location, the church was fortunate to lose only its dome to World War II bombing.

The rich marbled interior has well-lit side chapels and paintings of the saint that include Mattia Preti's *Martyrdom* work. There are valuable items shipped by the Knights from Rhodes; in the museum behind the church are Grand Master La Valette's hat and sword from the Great Siege victory celebrations in 1565. The church's large statue of St Lawrence is carried through the streets of the Three Cities on **Saint's Day**, 10 August.

The Gateways ★

Birgu's bastions have three imposing gateways constructed in the 1720s. Original road access was by the finely carved **Advanced Gate** and elegant **Couvre Porte**; it now goes through **Provence Gate.** By the old entrance to Vittoriosa is the small Malta at War Museum.

THE 100-TONNE GUN

The Armstrong 100-tonne gun, pointing out to sea above the Mediterranean Film Studios, is the world's largest muzzle-loading cannon and main feature of **Fort Rinella**, on the north coast beyond Kalkara. A Changing of the Guard ceremony is re-enacted there from time to time. The entrance to Rinella Battery can be found midway between the two gateways leading into the film studios.

KNOCK KNOCK

The home-proud Maltese take a particular pride in their front doorways, generally the first part of the house to be spruced up each day. Shining brass door knockers can take the form of a hand, a dolphin, an elephant's head, a fish or a Maltese cross; they make excellent souvenirs, as do the locally made porcelain house numbers. Ceramic wall plaques add a religious touch to the front of many homes.

Opposite top: *The fortifications on the peninsula of Senglea by night.*
Opposite bottom: *An eye for the invader on the vedette watchtower.*
Below: *The soaring dome of Our Lady of Victories parish church, Senglea, which has now been restored to its pre-war glory.*

SENGLEA

Senglea straddles the finger peninsula between Dockyard Creek and French Creek, facing Vittoriosa on the seaward side and the Corradino Heights inland. Protected by Fort St Angelo across Dockyard Creek, it developed from the mid-16th century, when French Grand Master **Claude de la Sengle**, who gave his name to the town, dispensed free plots for housing.

On the Vittoriosa side of Senglea, narrow stepped streets fall away to the water's edge; along the other side of the peninsula La Sengle's mighty fortifications extend round its tip into Dockyard Creek and continue inland, forming an impregnable barrier with Vittoriosa's own defences.

Church of Our Lady of Victories ★

Senglea was worst hit of the Three Cities in World War II and the rebuilt town shows little in common with L'Isla, as it was known at the time of the Knights. Among the buildings which suffered direct hits was the 17th-century parish church of Our Lady of Victories in the town's main square. The church was rebuilt by 1957 and interior painting of its dome finally completed in 1995 – a mighty edifice that rubs shoulders with some of Malta's highest-density housing just inside the city's main gate.

Inside are interesting Maltese paintings and a statue of Our Lady of Victories, which is borne through Senglea's streets on 8 September, **Victory Day**, remembering the Knights' Great Siege triumph and the end of World War II hostilities against Malta. The bell tower and dome at the end of Victory Street belong to the **Church of St Philip**, which despite its exposed position somehow escaped the bombing. The work of Maltese architect Carlo Valla, it dates from 1662.

Gardjola Garden ★★

At Senglea's furthest point, this delightful paved garden on the site of Fort St Michael affords the finest views of Valletta and Grand Harbour. To your right is mighty Fort St Angelo, and beyond the open sea; to your left, the distant derricks of Marsa; directly across the water the cream-coloured bastions that rise to the capital's Upper Barracca Gardens and Castile, flying the flag for the Prime Minister. From here you are in

no doubt that Valletta is a fortress city, built to be impregnable. Perched on the tip is the hexagonal **vedette**, a windowed watchtower with carved eye and ear to guard against the enemy.

Cospicua

The town of Cospicua, known as Bormla when it absorbed the overflow populace from the Knights' fortified base of Birgu, today links Senglea and Vittoriosa around the head of Dockyard Creek. The town's clustered streets nestle inside a double ring of bastions built to protect the Three Cities from threatened land attack.

Cotonera Lines ★★

It was in the mid-16th century that Bormla's growth called for new defences and in 1639 the Margherita Lines began to take shape. Six bastions were planned; three were completed quickly and the others by the 1730s. Work was interrupted when Grand Master **Nicolas Cotoner** pledged to fund an even stronger fortification and between 1670 and 1680 the Cotonera Lines were built, their eight mighty bastions and two demi-bastions strengthening 5km (3 miles) of defences and offering protection for 40,000 people and their animals. Included in the scheme was the construction of Fort Ricasoli.

A Unique Film Set

Close to Grand Harbour, for centuries the hub of Malta's seafaring activity, the modern Mediterranean Film Studios provide moviemakers with a unique sea setting. Two large circular water tanks, cleverly sited to show the sky as a backdrop, have been used in countless films and TV series – *Howards Way* and *Christopher Columbus* are examples. One tank is for surface filming and the other for shooting underwater scenes. The studios are close to Fort Ricasoli.

FORT RICASOLI

Two forts guard the narrow entrance to Grand Harbour – Fort St Elmo at the tip of Valletta and Fort Ricasoli just north of Kalkara on the Three Cities side. Fort Ricasoli was built in 1670 by Italian **Antonio Valperga**, responsible for the Cotonera Lines, and under the Knights it held a 2000-strong garrison. The fort was used as a set for the film *Troy*, complete with 12 m (38ft) high Trojan Horse, in 2003. A short distance away is **Fort St Rocco**, one of a number of smaller coastal defences that were erected by the Knights.

The defences were never tested – with a garrison of 8000 at the time of the French invasion in 1798, the Knights would have been hard-pressed to defend the Lines – and Bormla never grew to fill the enclosed area. Entry into the Three Cities was then, as now, through ornate gateways; impressive still is **Żabbar Gate**, a towering archway on the road from Żabbar bearing a bronze bust of Grand Master Nicolas Cotoner.

Like Senglea, Cospicua was devastatingly bombed in World War II, and much of it was turned to rubble. One building that survived against all the odds was the parish **Church of the Immaculate Conception**, built in 1637 and still standing proud within the close-knit dockyard community.

Kalkara ★

Through Salvatore Gate in the Cotonera Lines and outside the Three Cities, Kalkara hugs the quiet creek of the same name. It was known as English Creek in the Knights' era, when it sheltered galleys of the English *langue*. More modern than the Three Cities, having been largely rebuilt after World War II, Kalkara is dominated by the mighty façade of **St Joseph's Church**, itself completed in 1956, at the head of the creek.

Below: Żabbar Gate by the Three Cities.

On the headland of Mount Salvator beyond Kalkara is the one-time **Bighi Palace** of 1832, restored as the administration centre of the Malta Council for Science and Technology, a government advisory body. This and the adjacent colonnaded buildings were developed by the British as the **Bighi Naval Hospital** in the 19th century and remained as such until the British military presence ended in 1979. Beyond the small sandy bay used mainly by locals is **Fort Ricasoli**.

The Three Cities at a Glance

BEST TIMES TO VISIT

Like the capital Valletta, the Three Cities of Vittoriosa, Senglea and Cospicua are best visited outside the peak holiday months of July and August, when the temperature is more conducive to walking around their narrow streets and enjoying the superb cross-harbour views. Try to be there on **8 September** for the feast day of Our Lady of Victories, when a spectacular regatta in Grand Harbour celebrates the Knights' Great Siege victory and the end of World War II hostilities against Malta.

GETTING THERE

Though the Three Cities are a short *dgħajsa* trip across Grand Harbour from Valletta, most visitors will take the **road** through Marsa, signposted to the Three Cities. Other signs sometimes direct you to Birgu and Bormla, respectively the Knights' names for what are now Vittoriosa and Cospicua. The *dgħajsas* (high-prowed rowing boats more usually motor-driven nowadays) will take you to Senglea and Vittoriosa from Valletta's quayside – negotiate a price with the boatman.

Bus services to the Three Cities include: **1, 2, 6** Valletta–Cospicua–Vittoriosa; **3** Valletta–Fgura–Cospicua –Senglea; **4** Valletta–Cospicua –- Vittoriosa–Kalkara.

GETTING AROUND

If you manage to find one, a *dgħajsa* will ferry you across Dockyard Creek between Senglea and Vittoriosa. Once ashore, **walking** is the best way to explore the Three Cities – despite their grand name, they are but small towns easily traversed on foot. There are no taxi stands in the Three Cities.

WHERE TO STAY

There are no hotels, holiday apartments, guesthouses or similar in Vittoriosa, Senglea and Cospicua. Good news is that you are only 20 minutes' drive from Sliema, where there is a wide range of accommodation (*see* p. 57).

WHERE TO EAT

There is very little choice in the environs of the Three Cities. Two **kiosks** with outdoor seating on Senglea's promenade will serve you something-and-chips, but with one exception (*see below*) that is the nearest you'll get to *haute cuisine*. The kiosks stay open late, picking up trade after the open-air bingo session ends; they are worth at least a drink, if only for the view across Dockyard Creek to Vittoriosa's floodlit waterfront. There are one or two takeaway **pizzerias**, otherwise small bars frequented by locals might be able to rustle up a sandwich. For a **restaurant** meal, the best idea is to head west to Sliema or St Julian's, where

the choice is extensive. Or you can head in the opposite direction to Marsascala, a 15-minute drive away. **Bucintoro**, Casino di Venezia, Vittoriosa, tel: 2180 5580. Quality Italian restaurant on the top floor of Vittoriosa's waterfront casino.

TOURS AND EXCURSIONS

Half-day **coach tours** from Sliema and Buġibba take in the Three Cities, allowing time to visit the Maritime Museum and Inquisitor's Palace in Vittoriosa, the Cotonera Lines fortifications around Cospicua and Gardjola Garden overlooking Grand Harbour in Senglea. Two main operators with Three Cities tours are Josephine's, 80 The Strand, Sliema, tel: 2131 0435; and Nova Tours, Bay Square, Buġibba, tel: 2157 5240, 2157 5960. You can get a good close-up of the Three Cities on the Harbour cruise operated from the Strand at Sliema by Captain Morgan Cruises, tel: 2346 3333.

USEFUL CONTACTS

Tourist information, 1 City Gate, Valletta, tel: 2123 7747.
Police, tel: 191 (general inquiries 2122 4001).
St Luke's Hospital, tel: 2124 1251.
Airport (flight inquiries), tel: 2124 9600.
Taxi, tel: 2131 3261.

5
The South

This is rural Malta, a patchwork of postage stamp red-earth fields still tilled by hand and divided by rubble walls; of slow-moving donkey carts and an even slower pace of life. Along its heavily indented coastline are a series of appealing fishing villages, with bays populated by bright red, yellow, blue and green *luzzu* boats. Here too there is the juxtaposition of prehistoric temples and ancient caves beside the modern Freeport container terminal and new electricity generating station, with its obtrusive chimney, which virtually solved Malta's power supply problems overnight when it opened in 1992.

The southern region begins beyond the heavily developed area around Grand Harbour that embraces Marsa and the Three Cities. The small and bustling towns of **Paola** and **Fgura** extend the urbanization towards **Żabbar**; a bypass road sweeps round Żabbar's centre to reach the coast at **Marsascala**.

From Fort St Rocco by Grand Harbour, the rocky shore is deserted save for the tiny settlements of **Xghajra** and **San Pietru**. From Zonqor Point, one bay follows another through **Marsascala** and **St Thomas Bay** to **Marsaxlokk**, Malta's prettiest fishing village.

After **Birżebbuġa** at the far end of Marsaxlokk Bay, high limestone cliffs stretch more or less unbroken for the length of the island, cut only by the narrow, dried-up river valleys leading to **Blue Grotto** and **Għar Lapsi**.

Inland, villages huddle beneath huge churches. The smaller the village, it seems, the larger its church.

MEDITERRANEAN SEA

Żebbuġ · Gozo
· Victoria
Mġarr · Comino
Mellieħa · · Buġibba · Sliema
Għajn Tuffieħa · VALLETTA
Malta · Rabat · Hamrun · Żabbar
· Luqa
Birżebbuġa ·
· Żurrieq
MEDITERRANEAN SEA

DON'T MISS

★★★ **Blue Grotto:** fabulous reflections, but choose a calm day.
★★★ **Marsaxlokk:** picture-postcard fishing village.
★★★ **Hypogeum:** unique underground temple complex.
★★★ **Tarxien temples:** for a peep into the distant past.

Opposite: *Brightly painted* luzzu *fishing boats tied up in Marsaxlokk harbour.*

Above: *An excursion boat enjoys calm weather to explore the Blue Grotto.*

COASTLINE
Blue Grotto ★★★

Malta's rugged southern coast is pitted with sea caves, of which the Blue Grotto is the most spectacular. The 25-minute boat trip is best enjoyed in the early morning, when shafts of bright sunlight reflecting inside the cave turn the water several shades of vivid blue. Weather permitting, small boats holding up to eight passengers leave the rocky inlet by the fishing hamlet of **Wied-iż-Żurrieq**, with its handful of cafés and souvenir shops at the bottom of a scenic road from Żurrieq village. Though it sounds inviting, the Blue Grotto is in fact too inaccessible for swimming.

By another tiny cove is the small community of **Għar Lapsi**, also at the base of a steep road dropping from the cliff heights. A favourite of the Maltese and largely undiscovered by tourists, it has a no-frills café and good rock scrambles for the kids.

Għar Hasan ★

Hasan's Cave, at the end of a lane above Kalafrana, is entered from a path that affords spectacular views of the blue Mediterranean and has chambers opening on to the cliff face. It is where Hasan is said to have hidden in 1120 after the Saracens' expulsion from Malta. Alternatively, depending on which story you prefer, Hasan was a Turkish pirate who in 1578 took residence in the cave

and held Maltese women and girls captive there before they were shipped off to slavery in North Africa. One woman named Mary took the knife to him, thus ending five years of terror, and escaped from the cave – hence the story is there to be told. For a few cents, the lady in the hut by the car park will lend you a torch to see your way into the cave.

Għar Dalam **

Many of the dwarf elephant and hippopotamus that roamed 130,000 years ago over what is now Malta ended up in this long, tapering cave on the side of a dry river valley above Birżebbuġa. Excavations that started in 1865 have uncovered enough to fill every case in the small museum at the cave's entrance, including elephant molars, deer bones, antlers and hippo teeth. Their discovery fuelled speculation that the Maltese islands were once part of a land bridge between Europe and Africa.

Thousands of animals would have perished in the Stone Age cave, with the carcasses of many others washed there by floodwater. Some stumps of stalactites and stalagmites have survived and five distinct geological layers can be identified from the side-lit visitors' walkway running the length of the cave. Recent evidence indicates that the cave was used by Bronze Age man and later by the Phoenicians.

> **ALL THE SEVENS…**
>
> After Sunday lunch, or in the cool of the evening, village women gather to play *tombla* – open-air bingo. The numbers are called in English rather than Maltese; the cards are well worn, having been used hundreds of times; the counters are usually buttons. The womenfolk perch on ancient benches for their weekly gamble-and-gossip; the stakes are low and so are the prizes.

Below: *Exploring the depths of Għar Dalam, the 'cave of darkness'.*

TRY TWO WHEELS

If you are in Malta outside the hottest months, consider hiring a **bike** to do your sightseeing – it's a good way to get off the beaten track on lanes and tracks in the south of the island that are often inaccessible to cars. The all-terrain machines now available are particularly suited to Gozo's more remote parts. Cyclists should equip themselves with a decent map, as signposting is scarce or non-existent away from the towns and villages; distances are never given.

Below: *An aerial view of the Mnajdra temple site clearly shows the shape of the three temples.*

TARXIEN TEMPLES AND HYPOGEUM

The three Tarxien temples, believed to date from between 3000 and 1800BC, are among the most important evidence of the ancient cultures that once inhabited Malta. The temple site, now engulfed by urbanization, was discovered by a farmer in 1915.

In the first temple is a replica (the originals are in the National Museum of Archaeology in Valletta) of the base of a giant goddess statue, one of the world's earliest known representations of a deity. The second temple, with three chambers on either side of a central passage, is thought to have been used for the initiation of priests; it includes carvings of a bull and a sow with litter. Stone balls used to roll the massive temple slabs into place can also be seen. Early forms of cremation took place within these walls, evidenced by the darkly discoloured stone.

Ħal Saflieni Hypogeum ★★★

Malta's unique underground temple complex, discovered by chance in 1902 when builders were preparing a housing site in Paola, comprises a labyrinth of corridors and chambers on three levels, cut from the soft limestone between 4000 and 5000 years ago.

The upper level, 6m (20ft) below ground, dates from 3000BC; the other two levels, to a depth of 12m (40ft) at the foot of a modern staircase, were built around 2000BC to resemble surface temples elsewhere and so feature more ornate ceilings, walls and doorways. This was a place of both ancient worship and burial and at its lowest level the complex was found to contain a burial chamber with the remains of 7000 bodies.

The Holy of Holies chamber has strong architectural features and the red colouring of death on its walls – it was probably a shrine for the sacrifice of animals. Another, the oracle chamber, has outstanding acoustics and will reverberate a male – but not female – voice around its walls.

Ħaġar Qim and Mnajdra ★★

High on the southern clifftop between Għar Lapsi and the Blue Grotto, close to the village of Qrendi, are two more prehistoric temple sites. Ħaġar Qim, first excavated in 1839, occupies the higher ground; Mnajdra is a short way down the slope. Both face the open sea across to the islet of Filfla, which possibly had a ritualistic role in temple life that would explain the temples' remote location.

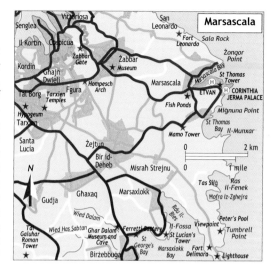

Ħaġar Qim (its simple translation is 'standing stones') used some of the largest slabs found in Maltese temple building, one a massive 7m by 3m (22ft by 10ft). The blocks were transported on the stone balls unearthed in some temples, but archaeologists remain baffled by how the larger ones were placed in their upright position. Ħaġar Qim's soft globigerina limestone walls have weathered badly, however, and later temple builders used the harder coralline limestone.

Mnajdra's three temples, within their protective coralline limestone wall, are in a better condition than Ħaġar Qim. The temples, dating from 2500BC, feature good corbelling and decorative work; a square-holed oracle chamber which was used by the priest can be clearly made out.

MARSASCALA ★★

The development of Marsascala from fishing village into small holiday resort followed the opening of the Jerma Palace Hotel around the headland in 1982. At that time a handful of waterfront bars and a couple of restaurants met the needs of day trippers; since then many more

ISLE OF FILFLA

Filfla, 5km (3 miles) offshore, is Malta's smallest island, measuring just 280m (910ft) by 50m (160ft) across its plateau. Sheer cliffs rising to 60m (195ft) render it inaccessible to all but experienced rock climbers. A small chapel existed on Filfla from the 14th to the 16th centuries; until 1971 the island was used for target practice by British warships and there are still unexploded bombs around its base. Since 1988 Filfla has been a Nature Reserve, with breeding colonies of the storm petrel, herring gull, Cory's shearwater and Manx shearwater.

THE SEASICK SUMMIT

Marsaxlokk Bay hosted one of the most remarkable meetings between heads of state in modern times. Here, aboard a naval ship, the **Bush–Gorbachev** summit between the Soviet and US leaders symbolically ended the Cold War, having been switched from Valletta for security reasons. In rough weather, the meeting, dubbed the 'seasick summit', was held in the bay between the Freeport and the power station on 2–3 December 1989. An ugly monument on Birżebbuġa seafront, paint-splattered and already badly weathered, commemorates the historic occasion.

have opened to cater for the rash of holiday apartments spreading towards St Thomas Bay. Now it is a popular night venue for the Maltese, who drive from all parts of the island at weekends to eat, drink and soak up the music in the seafront bars. Despite the building work, a wide promenade and its one-way traffic system, Marsascala clings on tenuously to its village atmosphere – a world apart from Sliema, St Julian's and, further up the coast, St Paul's Bay. The tranquillity, however, may not last much longer.

Next to the distinctive Libyan-owned Corinthia Jerma Palace Hotel – where Libyan leader Colonel Ghadaffi was an early visitor – is **St Thomas Tower**, built in 1614 by Grand Master Alof de Wignacourt after the Turks had landed in Marsascala Bay and sacked Żejtun. The fort, which was never attacked, was abandoned in 1798 when Malta fell to the French and has latterly seen use as a restaurant.

The coast road leads on to **St Thomas Bay**. Though villas and apartments edge the road, the bay with its outdoor café and stone fishermen's huts has remained largely unchanged over the years.

Below: *Fishermen on the quay at Marsaxlokk.*
Opposite: *Pretty Bay.*

MARSAXLOKK ★★★

While Marsascala has grown considerably to meet the increasing needs of tourism, only in recent years has Marsaxlokk made any such concessions. Thankfully, there are still no hotels or bland apartment blocks to disfigure Malta's most charming seaside village – just a scattering of fish restaurants and a few seafront bars that cater mainly for the many day trippers in the area.

Marsaxlokk (a corruption of the words for 'harbour' and 'sirocco', the warm winter wind that blows up from the Sahara) overlooks a bay packed in summer with traditional high-prowed *luzzu* fishing boats. Along the quayside, the Sunday morning market, selling everything from locally made lace tablecloths to freshly caught octopus, awakens the neighbours early and throughout the day attracts a succession of coach parties. South of the village, the early 17th-century St Lucien Tower, another Knights' stronghold, is now a marine laboratory.

Birżebbuġa *

A favoured landing place for enemy fleets in centuries past – the Turks before the Great Siege of 1565 and the French to terminate the Knights' rule in 1798 – Birżebbuġa has long been a summer resort for the Maltese. A lack of quality hotels and decent restaurants has isolated this small town from mainstream tourism. Dwarf palm trees fringe **Pretty Bay**, the south's only sandy beach of note, though thanks to the proximity of the Freeport it hardly justifies the name nowadays.

The resort spreads from compact **St George's Bay**, with small boats clustered behind its breakwater, through Pretty Bay to **Kalafrana** at the entrance to the vast **Malta Freeport** container terminal, which now processes some half-million containers annually. Near the most southerly point on the island is the redundant **Hal Far Airfield**, a legacy of World War II, now used for drag racing events.

SOUTHERN VILLAGES

Żurrieq, one of Malta's oldest parishes, is on the road to the Blue Grotto. The parish church of St Catherine dates from 1634 and contains fine works by Mattia Preti, who lived in the village in 1675. Several buildings from the Knights' era include the Armeria Palace, a former armoury.

COASTAL WALKS

While Malta's rocky foreshore is not ideal for serious hiking, there are good road walks along the coast. One from Valletta will take you past both Floriana and Marsamxett Harbour to Sliema and then St Julian's and St George's Bay. Another, from Marsascala, passes St Thomas Tower and St Thomas Bay before crossing the Delimara peninsula to Marsaxlokk; from here you can walk on to Birżebbuġa.

Above: Festa *time in Żurrieq. Flags and banners adorn the streets by St Catherine's parish church.*

The medieval Church of the Annunciation was built on the site of the long-abandoned Hal Millieri settlement.

Nearby **Qrendi** has three churches – the parish church of Santa Maria by Lorenzo Gafa (1685); St Catherine Tat-Torba, with its unusual façade added to an existing nave (1625); and St Saviour's, built in the style of a chapel. Near the latter is the Knights' late 16th-century Gwarena Tower, Malta's only octagonal defence.

Luqa, the site of Malta International Airport, was almost destroyed in World War II. The rebuilt parish church of St Andrew, originally dating from 1650, contains a Mattia Preti altarpiece. Nearer the new terminal is **Gudja**, birthplace of the architect Gerolamo Cassar, with the isolated **St Mary Ta' Bir Miftuħ**, dating from 1430 and one of the original 10 parish churches of Malta.

The road east from Gudja passes through **Għaxaq** to **Żejtun**, dominated by Lorenzo Gafa's massive parish church of St Catherine, the dome of which can be seen from afar. Much older is the former parish church of St Gregory, built in 1436 and enlarged by the Knights; the remains of more than 80 victims of a Turkish attack were discovered in passages there in the 1960s.

Żabbar, on the site of the camp established by the Turks before the Great Siege of 1565, boasts one of Malta's most unorthodoxly beautiful churches in the Sanctuary of the Virgin of Grace. This is Maltese Baroque at its most ornamental. It was started in 1641 and work continued over the next 100 years or so – hence some lack of harmony in design. On a roundabout on the Fgura side of town is the Hompesch Arch dedicated to the last Grand Master, Ferdinand de Hompesch.

The South at a Glance

BEST TIMES TO VISIT

Malta's southern part is best seen in **late spring**, if only for appreciating the island's greenery and admiring the wild flowers that colour the countryside between the scattered villages. It is amazing how quickly the scorching summer sun turns the landscape several shades of brown.

GETTING THERE

The southern areas of Malta are within easy reach of the Valletta–Sliema conurbation and roughly a half-hour's drive by **car** from the St Paul's Bay resort area. A large number of **bus routes** serve different parts of the area.

GETTING AROUND

A comprehensive **road** network links the towns and villages of Malta's south. Signposting has improved in recent years, but should you stray from the main roads, work out which direction you want to go and steer by the sun! A road tunnel beneath Malta International Airport's main runway links the communities north and south of the airport. The only road access to the sea on the southern coast is at Wied-iż-Żurrieq and Għar Lapsi. **Bus services**, mostly linking towns and villages in the area with Valletta, offer good connections around the region.

WHERE TO STAY

Corinthia Jerma Palace, Dawret it-Torri, tel: 2163 3222, fax: 2163 9485. Biggest and best in the south; distinctive four-star situated next to the sea on the edge of Marsascala.
Etvan, Bahhara Street, tel: 2163 2323, fax: 2163 4330. Friendly three-star hotel near the centre of Marsascala.

WHERE TO EAT

Hunters' Tower, Wilga Street, Marsaxlokk, tel: 2165 1792. More expensive seafront restaurant with good fish dishes and interesting range of starters.
Fisherman's Rest, St Thomas Bay, tel: 2163 2049. Off the tourist track, unpretentious, inexpensive and hard to beat for seafood.
Sottovoce, Marina Promenade, Marsascala, tel: 2163 2669. Good value Mediterranean with strong accent on seafood.
Langustini, Triq Id-Dahla, Ta' San Tumas, tel: 2163 9747. Large rooftop signage identifies long-established quality fish restaurant near St Thomas Bay.
Grabiel, Mifsud Bonnici Square, Marsascala, tel: 2163 4194. Nicely air-conditioned with a good Maltese mix.
L'Awwista, Zonqor Road, Marsascala, tel: 2163 2022. Mid-priced fish specialities overlooking the bay.
San Tomaso, St Thomas Bay, tel: 2163 9394. Alfresco dining in summer; a good spot to end your holiday.
Pisces, Xatt is-Sajjieda, Marsaxlokk, tel: 2165 4956. This restaurant is modern in style and has a splendid and inexpensive fish menu.
Is-Sajjied Restaurant, Xatt is-Sajjieda, Marsaxlokk, tel: 2165 2549. Serves a good antipasto selection and also fresh fish, mid-priced.

TOURS AND EXCURSIONS

Half-day and full-day **coach tours** from Sliema and Buġibba take in Malta's south, visiting Wied-iż-Żurrieq for boat trips to the Blue Grotto and the colourful fishing village of Marsaxlokk with its open-air market. The trips usually take in Marsascala and Birżebbuġa and often visit the stone quarries near Mqabba. Longer excursions visit the ancient temple sites at Tarxien and the prehistoric Għar Dalam cave. Leading operators with tours to the south are Josephine's, 80 The Strand, Sliema, tel: 2131 0435; and Nova Tours, Bay Square, Buġibba, tel: 2157 5240, 2157 5960.

USEFUL CONTACTS

Tourist information, 1 City Gate, Valletta, tel: 2123 7747.
Police, tel: 191 (general inquiries 2122 4001).
St Luke's Hospital, tel: 2124 1251.
Airport (flight inquiries), tel: 2124 9600.
Taxi, tel: 2131 3261.

6
Mdina and Rabat

Mdina was established by the Romans on a Bronze Age site as a settlement called **Melita** (meaning 'honey'), which was later fortified and renamed el-Medina ('city') by the Arabs. By the 16th century, after it had seen off Saracen raids, Mdina was the most sought-after place to live on Malta. High on a ridge in the centre of the island, it was easy to defend, while fertile land at its base provided food for those within. At the time of the **Great Siege** in 1565, it was the headquarters of the cavalry and when a force of 200 men rode forth from the city they were thought by the Turks camped at Marsa to be the feared reinforcements from Sicily – an error of judgement that led to the Turks' retreat and eventual downfall.

The Knights' decision to build Valletta as their new capital after the Great Siege diminished Mdina's importance – from being Citta Notabile, or Eminent City, it became Citta Vecchia, the Old City. Much later it became known as the **Silent City**, its narrow streets and alleyways uncluttered by motorcars, which are banned to all but residents.

At only 4ha (10 acres), Mdina is a city to wander in. Nowhere can so much rich history be packed into so small an area – palaces, a cathedral, churches, museums, a convent, small piazzas and houses of the Maltese aristocracy squeezed together inside the sturdy fortified walls and further protected by an enclosing dry moat. From the walls, the panorama across half of Malta to

DON'T MISS

*** **Mdina's Cathedral:** a masterpiece in Maltese Baroque architecture.
*** **A stroll in Mdina:** the best way to see the city – cars are banned anyway.
*** **Rabat's Catacombs:** rock-cut burial chambers of the early Christians.
* Tea at the **Fontanella tea garden:** an unrivalled setting.

Opposite: *From flowering fields in the centre of Malta rises the unmistakable shape of the city of Mdina.*

Above: *The ancient walls and spires of Mdina's skyline, dominated by the cathedral.*
Below: *The clock and bell tower on the cathedral.*

Grand Harbour and the Mosta Dome is unsurpassed. The city's own distinctive profile is Malta's crowning point, visible from much of the island.

Expansion beyond the city walls created the present town of **Rabat**; with its catacombs and Roman remains, it is older than Mdina and probably dates back to the Phoenicians. Rabat is the busy commercial hub of central Malta, with shops, bars and restaurants – and a marked contrast to the silent and brooding museum piece that is Mdina.

THE CATHEDRAL ★★★

One of Malta's treasures, Mdina's Baroque cathedral is dedicated to St Paul and shares the title of Co-Cathedral with St John's in Valletta. It was erected between 1697 and 1702 after the 1693 earthquake had all but destroyed the 13th-century original.

The distinguished Maltese architect **Lorenzo Gafa**, who strengthened and rebuilt parts of the old cathedral shortly before the earthquake struck, designed the new building that was to prove his masterpiece.

Within the grand and gilded interior, the many-coloured marble floor tablets, which identify the graves of important social and religious figures, are reminiscent of St John's Co-Cathedral. The apse, survivor of the earthquake with its 'Shipwreck of St Paul' mural by **Mattia Preti**, found a place in the new cathedral; also saved from the earthquake were the marble font and oak sacristy door.

High point in every respect is the cathedral's striking dome, a readily recognizable feature of the Mdina skyline, and widely regarded as Gafa's finest work. The inside of the dome was painted by **Mario Caffaro Rore** in 1955.

The cathedral's fine interior decorations include the nave ceiling fresco of 1794 by two Sicilian brothers, **Antonio** and **Vincenzo Manno**, depicting the life of St Paul. Other treasures are the Madonna icon, which some take to be the work of St Luke, in a side chapel; a silver medieval processional cross believed to have been brought by the Knights from Rhodes; and a communion chalice supposedly used by St Paul. The two early-17th century bronze cannon formally guarding the cathedral's entrance were returned to Malta from London at the insistence of the Governor in 1888.

Cathedral Museum ★★

Many artefacts salvaged after the earthquake are on display in the cathedral museum, which is housed in the seminary across Archbishop Square to the right of the cathedral. The building, a departure in style from other buildings of the period, is attributed to both Giovanni Barbara and Andrea Belli and dates from 1733.

In the museum are silver statues, outstanding Dürer engravings, paintings, manuscripts, lace and some 15th-century Sicilian choir panels.

> **MALTESE CHRISTMAS**
>
> The Maltese people make a lot of Christmas, dressing their houses and streets elaborately for the festive season. Nativity scenes adorn many front windows; cress is traditionally planted around the base of a crib containing a porcelain baby Jesus. In the south of the island, illuminated orange folded paper stars are hung in upstairs bay windows, their light glowing against a back curtain. Streets and churches in the towns and villages are hung with coloured lights that include the Maltese 'shooting star' decoration; many parishes have their own crib scene.

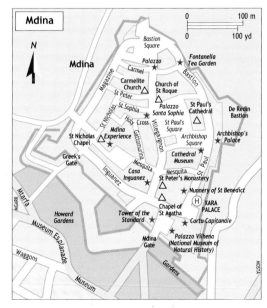

NORMAN HOUSE

On Villegaignon Street, near the Carmelite Church, is the **Palazzo Falzon**, with a slit-windowed lower section which dates from the 14th century. Sometimes called the **Norman House**, it is the only private house in Mdina open to the public and functions as a museum. Newly restored, it includes paintings, furniture, carpets, silver and more.

Above: *The courtyard of the Palazzo Falzon, a former nobleman's house.*
Opposite: *Mdina Gate, the main entrance into the Silent City.*
Below: *The labyrinthine alleyways of Mdina.*

AROUND MDINA
Streets, Walls and Gates

The walls enclosing Mdina and giving the Silent City its fortress appearance have their origins in Roman, Byzantine, Arab and Norman history, though it was the Knights who gave them their present form. The Arabs cut the ditch, today planted with orange trees, which the Knights widened into a dry moat that effectively isolated the citadel and cut Mdina to a third of its original size.

It was after the Great Siege and the development of Valletta that the Knights turned their attentions to the old capital. There are three ways into the city – through **Mdina Gate**, past the horse-drawn *karrozzini* standing for hire on the Rabat side of the bridge; via the **Greek's Gate** leading from the moat at the far end of Howard Gardens; and through a hole in the wall on the west side. The latter was cut early this century to give Mdina's citizens a short cut to the new railway station below the walls; the railway, alas, no longer exists.

The ornamental Baroque archway of the Mdina Gate

took its present form under Grand Master Manoel de Vilhena in 1724. The original access was at night across the drawbridge. At the same time the Greek's Gate, taking its name from the small Greek community who lived in the area, was similarly enhanced.

Mdina's main thoroughfare, **Villegaignon Street** – named after the French knight Nicolas Durand de Villegaignon (1510–71), who founded Rio de Janeiro – cuts from Mdina Gate to the high ramparts on the north side and is lined by most of the city's finest houses. To left and right as you amble through the quiet city, whose population of fewer than 400 rarely appear to venture outdoors, are narrow streets and gently curving alleyways, so designed to protect the inhabitants from attack and the buildings from the strong summer sun.

The street opens out into **St Paul's Square** before the great cathedral. Here there is a red telephone kiosk and postbox, legacies of British rule which show up brightly against the yellow stonework. Found at the far end of Villegaignon Street, behind the bulwark, is bougainvillea-flanked **Bastion Square**, with superb views across the Maltese landscape to St Paul's Bay, Grand Harbour and, in the middle distance, Mosta Dome and the National Stadium at Ta' Qali.

A Stroll in the Silent City ★★★

Entering through **Mdina Gate**, immediately on the right is the **Palazzo Vilhena**. It began life as the Magisterial Palace and was the inspiration of Maltese architect Giovanni Barbara in 1733; in 1909 it became the Connaught Hospital of the British and is now the **National Museum of Natural History**.

To the left is the 16th-century **Tower of the Standard**, which formerly served as Mdina's police station, now opposite.

> ### MALTA'S RAILWAY
>
> Malta enjoyed a brief flirtation with the railway age. The Malta Railway Company was formed in 1880 and on 1 March 1883 it opened a line between Valletta and Mdina. Traffic was poor, however, and the Maltese administration took over the line in 1890. It ran profitably until competition from the Valletta– Birkirkara tramway, which started up in 1905, and buses caused its demise. Planned extensions to Sliema, Mosta and Żebbuġ never materialized and, unable to sustain further losses, the railway closed on 1 April 1931.

Its function has always been to protect the populace – originally fires were lit aloft to warn the citizens of an impending invasion. Directly ahead across **St Publius Square** is **St Peter's Monastery**, home of the Benedictine nuns, rebuilt in 1625 but 200 years older. The nuns are of a strict order that decrees they must be buried within the precincts; the only men allowed inside are the doctor, decorator, lawyer and undertaker – and then only with the bishop's permission.

Opposite the nunnery, at No. 3 Villegaignon Street, is imposing **Casa Inguanez**, the home since 1350 of Mdina's oldest family and once the hereditary governors of the city. The oldest house in Mdina – and reputedly in Malta – is **Palazzo Santa Sophia**, found on the left hand side of Villegaignon Street just past the cathedral by Holy Cross Street.

The large church on the left is the **Carmelite Church** and priory. Villegaignon Street opens on to **Bastion Square**; to your right, tucked inside the northern wall, the **Fontanella tea garden** is one of Mdina's most spectacularly situated eating places. The tea and cakes are excellent.

RABAT

For most visitors, Rabat exists as an add-on to Mdina – a place to visit only for its catacombs. Yet it exudes character in its confined streets of shops and town houses and deserves more attention. It is looked on as the suburb of Mdina; before the Arabs reduced Mdina's size the roles were reversed. Rabat's development has been accompanied by commercial growth and today it prospers alongside, rather than because of, Mdina.

The Catacombs ★★★

Rabat has a vast network of catacombs and two in St Agatha Street are open to visitors. The most extensive, **St Paul's Catacombs**, are a labyrinth of tunnels, niches and rock tombs in use up to the 4th century AD. **St Agatha's Catacombs** are below the church dedicated to the saint, who fled to Malta from Catania in AD249 to escape persecution and is believed to have hidden in the underground cemetery before returning to Sicily to die a martyr.

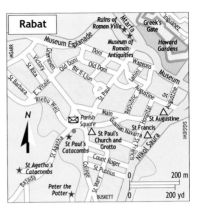

Rabat

As their belief that the dead should be buried conflicted with Roman law stipulating cremation, Malta's Christians adopted the burial method of the Palestinian Jews by carving these vast labyrinths. Family graves are cut into the rock walls; there are also stone canopies, benches and early communion tables used by the early Christians. Just visible on some tombs are the remains of frescoes.

St Paul's Church and Grotto ★★

On Rabat's Parish Square, site of Malta's first Christian community, the 16th-century, cross-shaped parish **Church of St Paul** ranks among the country's most impressive edifices – a product of the new prosperity

POPE'S VISIT

On his 1990 visit to Malta, Pope John Paul II held prayers in the grotto beneath St Paul's church in Rabat. On a plaque outside the church on College Street is his parting 'God Bless Malta' prayer said at the airport. The yellow and white colours of the Vatican fluttered from every flagpole throughout the islands during his visit; many of these flags are still unfurled on special festive occasions.

Left: *St Paul's Catacombs, largest of Rabat's ancient burial complexes.*
Opposite: *Ornate design high above Villegaignon Street in Mdina.*

THE MNARJA RACES

Rabat plays a big part in the festival on 29 June of St Peter and St Paul – the Mnarja (it derives from the Latin word *illuminaria,* to light up). The bareback horse and donkey races on the steep Saqqajja hill leading into Rabat from Valletta have been held since the time of the Knights. Winners are handed banners called *palji* from a loggia at the winning post; they are used as altar cloths for the following year. The feast of Mnarja also comes alive in Buskett Gardens, where crowds gather for a day of high revelry.

Below: *An outstanding example of mosaic work in the Roman Villa and Museum at Rabat. A Roman town flourished in the vicinity.*

generated by the Knights. Though it dates from 1575, the church was largely rebuilt in the late 17th century and bears the hallmark of Lorenzo Gafa. The main altar-piece is by Mattia Preti.

Beneath the church is the **Grotto of St Paul**; according to tradition the Apostle lived and preached or was imprisoned in it during his winter in Malta. The cave's walls reputedly have the power of healing and it is said that no matter how much stone is scraped away by those seeking a cure, the cave's size never alters. The grotto contains a marble statue of St Paul, sculpted by Michelangelo's assistant Bernini and brought from Rhodes by Grand Master Manuel Pinto de Fonseca. In the early 1600s the cave was home to a Spanish nobleman, Giovanni Beneguas, who arrived to join the Knights but instead chose to live as a hermit and used his wealth to build the adjacent **Church of St Publius**. Across College Street in Wignacourt College is the small **St Paul's Museum**, with a miscellany of early finds.

St Augustine's Church, with its Renaissance-style façade, which is situated just off the town centre, was built by Gerolamo Cassar in 1571 and was his first church of major significance, preceding his Co-Cathedral in Valletta by just two years.

Roman Villa and Museum ★★

At the far end of Howard Gardens, by the Greek's Gate leading into Mdina, a small neoclassical museum encloses the mosaic floor of a Roman villa and displays other Roman antiquities. The remains of the villa, among Malta's most significant Roman legacies and probably the home of a wealthy merchant, were discovered in 1881.

Mdina and Rabat at a Glance

BEST TIMES TO VISIT

Mdina is best visited out of the peak holiday months of July/August, when there are fewer holiday-makers in its narrow streets and alleyways. Go early or late in the day to avoid the crowds. Take in Rabat in **late June** if you can, when the Mnarja horse and donkey races are held as part of the festival of St Peter and St Paul.

GETTING THERE

Mdina and Rabat sit in the centre of the island, within easy reach of Valletta, Sliema and St Paul's Bay. **Road** access is good from all parts of the island. **Bus** services to Mdina and Rabat include: **65** from Sliema; **80**, **81** from Valletta; **84** from Mtarfa; **86** from Buġibba.

GETTING AROUND

Car use in Mdina is restricted to residents; the large car park outside the main gateway into the walled city usually has empty places and you can park all day for a few cents. Mdina is no place for cars anyway, as streets in the tiny city are narrow and usually packed with pedestrians. Horse-drawn *karrozzini* are allowed, however, and will give you a guided tour of both Mdina and neighbouring Rabat for a modest fee. Parking places are usually available down the hill facing St Paul's Church.

WHERE TO STAY

Xara Palace, Mdina, tel: 2145 0560, fax: 2145 2612. Five-star luxury in 17-room former palace by Mdina's city wall. **Point de Vue**, The Saqqajja, Rabat, tel: 2145 4117. Character guest house in 17th-century building; great views.

WHERE TO EAT

Eating places in Mdina tend to cater for those requiring either a full dinner or just tea and cakes – there's not much of a choice in between and Rabat is even shorter on restaurants. **Cosmana Navarra**, St Paul's street, Rabat, tel: 2145 0638. Baroque-style restaurant serving Med/Maltese dishes near St Paul's Church.
Bacchus, Inguanez Street, Mdina, tel: 2145 4981. Former munitions magazine and wine cellar within Mdina's fortifications offering a classy menu in the upper price range.
Medina, Holy Cross Street, Mdina, tel: 2145 4004. Sophisticated dining in the Silent City.
Il Veduta, The Saqqajja, Rabat, tel: 2145 4666. Pizza, fish and grills on terrace near Mdina Gate.
Trattoria AD 1530, Mdina, tel: 2145 2612. Light and sophisticated fare in atmospheric Xara Palace Hotel trattoria.
Fontanella, Bastion Street, Mdina, tel: 2145 4264. Light meals atop the bastions; afternoon tea with a huge cake list.
Ciappetti, St Agatha's Esplanade, Mdina, tel: 2145

9987. Outstanding Italian-Maltese restaurant with views from the bastions.

TOURS AND EXCURSIONS

Full-day and half-day **coach tours** are operated from Sliema and Buġibba to Mdina and Rabat. Time is allowed for a guided walk through the streets of the Silent City that includes a visit to the cathedral and Cathedral Museum; also a walk along the ramparts that offers splendid views across the island. Most tours also take in St Paul's and St Agatha's Catacombs, Grotto of St Paul and Roman Villa and Museum in Rabat. Two principal operators featuring tours of Mdina and Rabat are: Josephine's, 80 The Strand, Sliema, tel: 2131 0435; and Nova Tours, Bay Square, Buġibba, tel: 2157 5240, 2157 5960. Attractions presenting Mdina's colourful history are the **Mdina Dungeons** in St Publius Square, tel: 2145 0267; the **Mdina Experience** in Mesquita Square, tel: 2145 4322; **Medieval Times** in the Palazzo Costanzo, tel: 2145 4625; **Tales of the Silent City** in Villegaignon Street, tel: 2145 1179; and **Knights of Malta** in Magazine Street, tel: 2145 1342.

USEFUL CONTACTS

Tourist information, 1 City Gate, Valletta, tel: 2123 7747. **Police**, tel: 191 (general inquiries 2122 4001). **St Luke's Hospital**, tel: 2124 1251.

7
The Centre

The central part of Malta, dotted with small towns and villages and crisscrossed by narrow country lanes, is defined by the Victoria Lines escarpment to the west, the concentrated urbanization of Valletta's various satellite towns and suburbs to the east and the Dingli Cliffs to the south.

The unmissable highlight in a tour of the centre is medieval **Mdina** (see p. 79). Beside the Victoria Lines are **Mosta** and **Naxxar**, and grouped in the geographical centre of the island is the prime residential area of the **Three Villages** – Attard, Lija and Balzan – with green San Anton Gardens between them. Nearer Valletta are the lively **commercial** centres of Birkirkara and Ħamrun; to the south of the **urban** area Qormi, Żebbuġ and Siġġiewi; and way out towards the southern cliffs the village of **Dingli**, with the green oasis of Buskett Gardens in the lee of Verdala Palace.

MOSTA **

The buzzing little town of Mosta is best known for the **Church of St Mary**, usually called simply either the **Mosta Dome** or the **Rotunda**, and visible from a large part of the island. At 37m (122ft) across, it is Europe's third largest unsupported dome, built between 1833 and 1860 in the style of the Pantheon and surpassed in size only by St Peter's in Rome and St Sophia's in Istanbul. Taller, but slightly narrower is the modern St John's Church at Xewkija in Gozo (see p. 117).

DON'T MISS

*** Mosta Dome:** its sheer size will not fail to impress.
** Ta' Qali Craft Centre:** great for gifts and souvenirs.
** Buskett Gardens:** some welcome greenery close to Verdala Palace.
** San Anton:** attractive formal gardens by the President's palace.

Opposite: *Mosta is dominated by its church; its mighty dome can be seen across the island.*

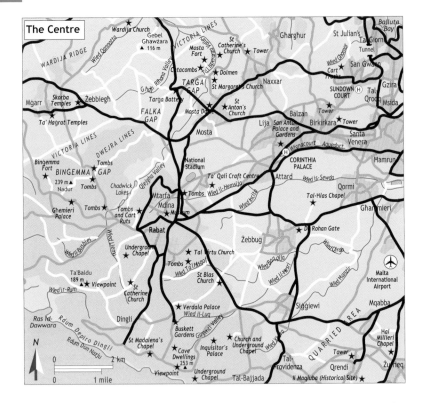

The Rotunda was built by volunteer labour, completed without the use of scaffolding and financed entirely by the local parish. On display is the casting of the World War II bomb that fell through the roof and rolled across the floor during a service but miraculously failed to explode. Just west of Mosta is the **Chapel of Tal L'Isperanza**, typical of the tiny wayside chapels found in more remote parts of the Maltese countryside.

Naxxar ★

A neighbour of Mosta, Naxxar hosts Malta's annual International Fair in early July. It is one of the island's oldest parishes, dating from the mid-1400s; the parish church of **Our Lady of Victories**, completed in 1616, was

Tomasso Dingli's work, though the façade and side aisles were 20th-century additions. Dingli also designed the **Church of St Bartholomew** in Għargħur.

Watchtowers commanding the heights towards the Victoria Lines include **Gauci's Tower** in adjoining San Pawl Tat-Tarġa (meaning St Paul's steps), where it is believed the Apostle preached.

Above: *The Classical frontage of the Mosta Rotunda.*

Ta' Qali ★★

Situated on the former World War II airfield, **Ta' Qali Craft Centre** is Malta's largest local craft market. Craftsmen can be seen at work and their silver filigree jewellery, the famous coloured Mdina glassware, ceramics, wicker furniture, wrought ironwork and items of Malta stone are all produced on site and well displayed. Prices here are generally lower than in seaside souvenir shops.

Nearby rises the modern **Ta' Qali Stadium**, home of Malta's national soccer team and venue for the programme of matches in the island's Premier League. Here too is the **Malta Aviation Museum**, housed in two former RAF huts and other buildings – it includes early aircraft, engines, memorabilia and models.

THE THREE VILLAGES ★

The villages of Lija, Balzan and Attard contain many of the island's most desirable residences, some of which go back to the 17th century. **Lija's** reputation for having the best *festa* is well founded. It takes place around 8 August each year and is centred on the parish church of St Saviour. The church, with some fine frescoes, was completed in 1694 to designs by Giovanni Barbara and is widely regarded as his best work – he was only 24 at the time. Lija's Old Parish Church, built in the 16th century, is in St Saviour's Street; between them is the little Church of St Peter, dating from 1728.

MALTESE BREAD

Malta's excellent crusty bread has its origins with the bakeries established by the Knights. Their recipes exist today with few modifications – the flat *ftira* bread is still popular while larger loaves have a thick crust and nutty flavour. **Qormi** is reputed to produce the best bread and at one time was known as the village of the bakers; in some towns and villages you can buy bread hot from a wood-burning oven.

Above: *A blaze of colour in San Anton Gardens, known for their variety of unusual trees and plants.*

In **Balzan's** main square, the Baroque parish Church of the Annunciation, from the late 17th century, has a decidedly Spanish appearance. On Three Churches Street are the small Church of St Roque, built in 1723 and dedicated to the protector of plague victims; the 15th-century Little Church of the Annunciation; and a small former church now in private hands.

Like Lija, **Attard** has a parish church designed by a man in his twenties – Tomasso Dingli was just 22 when he completed the Church of St Mary in 1616. Malta's finest Renaissance building, it has an excellent carved façade based on a Roman temple front.

The Three Villages are grouped around the lush greenery of **San Anton Gardens**, next to the Presidential Palace. The gardens, planned in the 17th century, provide a shady retreat in summer and contain some unusual species. There is also a small zoo.

THE CENTRAL TOWNS
Birkirkara ★

Often called B'kara, this is the largest of the towns and villages contributing to the urban and industrial sprawl west of Valletta. It is a typically Maltese working town, still showing its village origins in a centre dating from the 16th century.

The shining glory of Birkirkara is its tall Baroque parish **Church of St Helena**, designed by Maltese architect Domenico Cachia and built between 1735 and 1745. Cachia fashioned St Helena at the age of 27 and was later responsible for the brilliant rebuilding of the Auberge de Castile et Leon in Valletta. St Helena's external features include two attractive bell towers; the interior is richly gilded and carved, with excellent frescoes.

The **Church of the Annunciation**, the former parish church, had fallen into serious disrepair by the 1970s but is now restored. It was built in 1617 by Vittorio Cassar, son of better-known architect Gerolamo Cassar.

Ħamrun ★

The old town of Ħamrun, with its long main street of

tiny shops, sits astride the Rabat road 2km (1¼ miles) from Valletta. Its small chapel of **St Mary of Porto Salvo** dates from 1736. In nearby **Santa Venera** is the country villa of **Casa Leoni,** with its outstanding formal gardens built in 1730 for Grand Master Manoel de Vilhena.

Qormi ★

Once called Casal Fornaro (village of the bakers), Qormi has a long tradition for producing Malta's delicious crusty bread (*see* p. 90), though the old ways of baking are gradually giving way to more modern methods. Some fine buildings line its old streets, such as the **Stagno Palace** of 1589 in Dun Marigo Street and the parish **Church of St George**, which has an elegant Renaissance façade.

Żebbuġ ★

Between Qormi and Żebbuġ, standing alone in the fields, is the small **Tal-Ħlas Chapel**, designed by Lorenzo Gafa in 1690. The entrance into Żebbuġ is through the **De Rohan Gate**, built in 1677 and a century later named after French Grand Master Emanuel de Rohan-Polduc. Inside the small town, which at one time had a reputation for producing sailcloth, are some fine houses of the 17th and 18th centuries and several interesting churches. Most imposing is the parish **Church of St Philip**, built in 1599 with similarities to St John's Co-Cathedral in Valletta; others are the **Chapel of St Roque** from 1593, the 18th-century **Our Lady of Angels** and the **Chapel of Tal-l'Abbundunata** from 1758.

Siġġiewi ★

The village of Siġġiewi is dominated by its splendid parish **Church of St Nicholas**, the inspiration of Lorenzo Gafa and built in 1675. It is widely held to be Malta's finest Baroque church and boasts one of the highest domes on the island.

THE GLASSBLOWERS

Malta's coloured glassware makes one of the best-value and most distinctive souvenirs of the islands – and you can see it in the making. At **Mdina Glass**, on the edge of Ta' Qali Craft Centre, a giant shed houses the furnaces where craftsmen skilfully turn the molten glass into vases, bottles, ornaments and paperweights. The items come in an assortment of colours, but predominantly the attractive blue-green for which Mdina Glass is famous. There are bargains to be picked up on the seconds counter. Other manufacturers are **Phoenician Glass**, on Manoel Island at Sliema, and **Gozo Glass**, at Gharb on Gozo.

Below: *Towering Dingli Cliffs on Malta's scenic southern shore.*

CLAPHAM JUNCTION

Named after the busiest railway intersection in Great Britain, Clapham Junction on Malta is a major confluence of prehistoric 'cart ruts' near Buskett Gardens. Mysterious parallel grooves in the rock surface, they are believed to have been part of an early transportation system. Whether the ruts were carved by animal-hauled sledge or wheeled vehicle, or whether they were deliberately cut remains open to conjecture. What is surprising is that some lead straight over the cliff edge. You will need to look hard to locate them. There are similar cart ruts elsewhere in Malta and at Sannat in Gozo.

Below: *Verdala Palace overlooks the verdant Buskett Gardens, with their plantations of firs, cypress, oaks and citrus trees.*

DINGLI ★

Dingli, Malta's highest village with houses clustered round its silver-domed church, is best known for its cliffs. The small village is 1km (⅔ mile) from the dramatic Dingli Cliffs that tumble down 253m (820ft) through cultivated terraces to the blue Mediterranean below. Some 5km (3 miles) offshore is the islet of Filfla (*see* p. 73).

The clifftops make fine walking country. Near the highest point is the **Madalene Chapel**, possibly the most isolated building in the Maltese islands and open only on 22 July, the Feast of St Magdalene. A wall plaque informs those seeking sanctuary from the law that they will not find it there – a warning dating from the early 17th century, when the Knights sought to restrict the protection afforded by the church.

Verdala Palace ★★

Overlooking the lush greenery of Buskett Gardens, Verdala Palace was built in 1586 as a luxurious summer retreat for extrovert French cardinal Grand Master **Hugues Loubenx de Verdalle**. It was designed by **Gerolamo Cassar** as a fortified castle and today, as the official summer residence of the President, it is used to host visiting VIPs. A flight of steps crosses the moat from which was cut the palace's building stone; inside a superb elliptical staircase in one corner leads to the first floor. The great hall contains frescoes of Verdalle's life, while in the first-floor dining room is the chess board chiselled out of the stone floor by French prisoners in 1812.

Buskett Gardens ★★

This delightfully green area, last vestige of the forest that once covered Malta, is popular for its flora in spring and its wooded shade in summer. The name stems from the Italian *boschetto* (little wood). In late June big crowds gather here for the **Mnarja** festival.

The Centre at a Glance

BEST TIMES TO VISIT

The centre of Malta is best enjoyed in **late spring**, when you can appreciate the island's rural aspects and admire the wild flowers, especially in the fields below Mdina's citadel and on the high Dingli cliffs. If you are there in summer, the thick tree coverage of Buskett Gardens provides shady relief from the powerful sun.

GETTING THERE

Malta's central area is within easy reach by **road** of Malta's main centre of Valletta and Sliema, the St Paul's Bay resort district and the hotels of the north. The **bus** connections to the south include: **40** Valletta–Balzan–Lija– Attard; **43**, **44**, **45**, **47**, **49**, **50**, **52**, **53**, **57** Valletta– Birkirkara–Balzan–Mosta; **54**, **56** Valletta–Balzan– Naxxar; **55** Valletta–Naxxar– Għargħur; **65** Sliema–Mosta– Ta' Qali–Rabat; **74** Valletta– San Anton–Attard; **81** Valletta– Rabat–Buskett–Dingli; **88** Valletta–Qormi–Żebbuġ; **89**, **90**, **91** Valletta–Qormi.

GETTING AROUND

A comprehensive **road** network links the towns and villages of Malta's central area. Though road signage has improved in recent years, it may be difficult finding directions if you stray from the main roads outside the built-up areas on to the network of lanes crisscrossing the countryside. There is no road access to the sea on Malta's southern coast west of Għar Lapsi; the road that runs along the top of Dingli cliffs affords some fine views out to sea towards the islet of Filfla. **Bus** services, linking towns and villages in the area with Valletta, offer good connections within the region.

WHERE TO STAY

Malta's central region has only two hotels, both five-star – the Xara Palace in Mdina (*see* p. 87) and the Corinthia Palace. There are no holiday apartments in the area. Plenty of hotel and self-catering accommodation can be found by the coast in the Sliema/St Julian's area and in the St Paul's Bay resorts.
Corinthia Palace, tel: 2144 0301, fax: 2146 5713. Five-star elegance in one of Malta's few inland hotels, situated by San Anton Gardens. Opened by the Duke of Edinburgh in 1968, it contains a health spa.

WHERE TO EAT

There aren't too many places to go if you get hungry in middle Malta. The Corinthia Palace Hotel and a selection of eating places in Mdina (*see* p. 87) are the best bet, plus one beyond Dingli and one in Mosta. Do-it-yourself pick-nickers should try Qormi, the village of the bakers, for a crusty loaf, perhaps with local goat's cheese and washed down with a bottle of Maltese wine.
Bobbyland, Panoramic Road, Dingli, tel: 2145 2895. Reasonably priced Maltese specialities at this eatery on Dingli cliffs.
Ta' Marija, Constitution Street, Mosta, tel: 2143 4444. Mid-Malta restaurant recommended for its local specialities.

TOURS AND EXCURSIONS

Half-day and full-day **coach tours** operate from Malta's principal resort areas to attractions in the centre of the island. Among sites visited are the Ta' Qali Craft Centre, where time is allowed for shopping and watching craftsmen at work, the Malta Aviation Museum at Ta' Qali and Mosta Dome. Tours to the region also visit the green areas of San Anton Gardens and Buskett Gardens. Two of the leading operators with tours that take in the centre of the island are Josephine's, 80 The Strand, Sliema, tel: 2131 0435; and Nova Tours, Bay Square, Buġibba, tel: 2157 5240, 2157 5960.

USEFUL CONTACTS

Tourist information, 1 City Gate, Valletta, tel: 2123 7747.
Police, tel: 191 (general inquiries 2122 4001).
St Luke's Hospital, tel: 2124 1251.

8
The North

Malta's northern region, though often remote and detached from the rest of the island by the Victoria Lines escarpment, has developed as a significant tourist area around **St Paul's Bay**, named after the Apostle's well-chronicled shipwreck of AD60. The twin resorts of **Buġibba** and **Qawra** link hands across the Qawra peninsula that separates St Paul's Bay and Salina Bay – the streets of both are packed with holiday apartments and hotels. Beyond Buġibba is the original fishing village of St Paul's Bay, now enmeshed in the coastal development that extends onwards past **Xemxija Bay**, the innermost reach of St Paul's Bay, and up the steep hill to overlook the Mistra Valley.

The bays and inlets of the north contain almost all of Malta's sandy beaches – from the wide expanse of Mellieħa Bay to the sand of aptly named Golden Bay on the opposite coast and other stretches of beach beyond the Marfa Ridge.

ST PAUL'S BAY

The generous sweep of St Paul's Bay is Malta's second holiday area after Sliema and St Julian's. It tends to include Qawra, although most of that town is around the headland facing Salina Bay.

The coast road hugging Malta's barren northern shore from the Mediterraneo Marine Park at Baħar iċ-Ċagħaq to **Salina Bay** leads past the Coastline Hotel and then the long-disused but still pungent **salt pans** cut by the

DON'T MISS

** **Popeye Village:** tumble-down Sweethaven brought back to life at Anchor Bay.
** **Victoria Lines:** renovated century-old defences built by the British.
** **Għajn Tuffieħa Bay:** arguably the prettiest of Malta's sandy bays.
** **San Pawl il Baħar:** the little fishing village of St Paul's Bay.

Opposite: *Excursion boats alongside St Paul's Bay jetty at Buġibba. Trips take in the bays of northern Malta and Comino.*

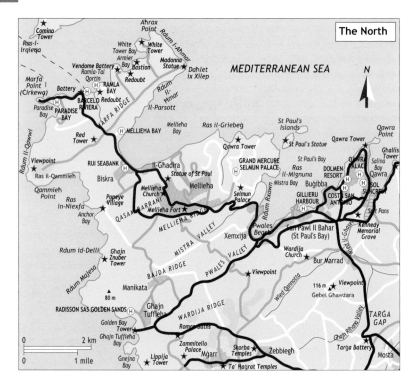

The North

Map labels:
Comino Tower, Ras-l-Irqieqa, Ahrax Point, Rdum l-Ahmar, White Tower Bay, White Tower, Armier Bay, Madonna Statue, Bastion, Dahlet ix Xilep, MEDITERRANEAN SEA, N, Vendome Battery, Ramla-Tal Qortin, Redoubt, Marfa Point (Cirkewg), Battery, RAMLA BAY, Rdum il-Hmar, BARCELO Redoubt, RIVIERA, Paradise Bay, PARADISE BAY, Il-Parsott, MARFA RIDGE, Rdum il-Qawwi, Mellieha Bay, Ras il-Griebeg, St Paul's Islands, Qawra Point, Red Tower, MELLIEHA BAY, Qawra Tower, St Paul's Statue, Qawra Tower, Qawra Point, Viewpoint, RUI SEABANK, Il-Ghadira, GRAND MERCURE SELMUN PALACE, St Paul's Bay, Ghallis Tower, Ras il-Qammieh, Biskra, Statue of St Paul, Ras il-Mignuna, DOLMEN RESORT, Salina Bay, Qawra, Qammieh Point, Ras in-Niexfa, Mellieha Church, Mellieha, Mistra Bay, Buġibba, GILLIERU HARBOUR, QAWRA PALACE, SOL SUNCREST, COSTA SAN ANTONIO, Anchor Bay, Popeye Village, QASAM BARRANI, Mellieha Fort, Selmun Palace, Rdum Rxawn, Salt Pans, Rdum id-Delli, Ghajn Znuber Tower, MELLIEHA RIDGE, Xemxija, Pwales Beach, San Pawl Il Bahar (St Paul's Bay), Wardija Church, Kennedy Memorial Grove, Il-Ghasel Path, Rdum Majesa, MISTRA VALLEY, BAJDA RIDGE, PWALES VALLEY, Bur Marrad, Wied Qannotta, Manikata, 80 m, Viewpoint, 116 m, Viewpoint, Gebel Ghawżara, RADISSON SAS GOLDEN SANDS, Ghajn Tuffieha, WARDIJA RIDGE, Ghajn Rihana Valley, TARĠA GAP, Golden Bay Tower, Roman Baths, Ghajn Tuffieha Bay, Zammitello Palace, Mġarr, Skorba Temples, Żebbiegh, Targa Battery, Mosta, Gnejna Bay, Lippija Tower, Ta' Hagrat Temples, 0　2 km, 0　1 mile

Knights. Just off the road is the **Kennedy Grove** memorial to the assassinated US President, now sadly unkempt and in need of attention. The Maltese, with the best of intentions, erect monuments to the fallen and worthy but then tend to forget about them and frequently allow them to fall into a state of disrepair.

Qawra ★

To the north lies Qawra which, before the building of the Qawra Palace and Suncrest hotels in the mid-1980s gave it a shot in the arm, was a quiet resort of scattered aparthotels and holiday apartments. Behind the seafront apartments development is still proceeding, and one questions whether lessons have been learned from the sporadic and haphazard growth of Buġibba.

Buġibba ★

The souvenir shops start immediately past the Dolmen Resort Hotel. This is Buġibba, despised by locals for its un-Maltese appearance but a place that welcomes many thousands of low-budget holiday-makers each year. Throughout the 1980s Buġibba resembled a building site as developers, having sought to cash in on the tourism boom of the late 1970s, ran out of money. Now most of the work has been completed, though the end result is hardly beautiful and the whole sadly lacks planning. Alongside such long-standing enterprises as the Tartan Bar and Bognor Regis, a large seafront café, there is a rash of fast-food outlets, bars and mini-markets that testify to the resort's popularity.

Above: *St Paul's Bay is one of several fishing harbours dotted about Malta.*

San Pawl Il Baħar ★★

After the brash, the beautiful. The old fishing harbour of St Paul's Bay, with its brightly painted *luzzu* craft and neat little church, is a treat after featureless Buġibba. The **Church of St Paul**, open only in summer, was given its distinctive arcade in the 17th century and bears panels of New Testament quotations in several languages relating to St Paul's time in Malta. Dominating the little harbour, but not too intrusive, is the Gillieru Harbour Hotel.

The restored **Wignacourt Tower**, built by Grand Master Alof de Wignacourt in 1610, overlooks the harbour. Across the bay beyond Xemxija is the coastal indentation of **Mistra Bay**, where a former abandoned farmhouse, reputedly a haunt of smugglers, has been converted into an upmarket restaurant.

> ### ST PAUL IN MALTA
>
> St Paul and his fellow prisoners were welcomed ashore after their shipwreck. The **Church of St Paul** in San Pawl Il Baħar is said to be on the site where St Paul shook off a deadly viper into the fire and won over the islanders. The spring of **Għajn Razul**, or **Apostle's Fountain**, is supposedly where St Paul struck a rock to provide drinking water for the survivors. St Paul spent three months in Malta, preaching the Gospel (he converted the Roman governor Publius to Christianity) and healing the sick before continuing his journey via Syracuse to Rome.

UNDERWATER SAFARIS

If you fancy exploring the deep without getting your hair wet, the Underwater Safari boat of the **Captain Morgan** company operates several cruises daily from the small quay at Buġibba. A sophisticated improvement on the glass-bottomed boat, the Underwater Safari craft accommodates passengers in a glass-sided lounge below deck that affords excellent views of marine life through the crystal clear water.

Mellieħa Bay ★★

This is Malta's largest beach, 600m (⅓ mile) long and resplendent with bright umbrellas in summer, when it throngs with local families and tourists. Dinghies, pedaloes and windsurfers are available for water-sports fans; a succession of no-frills beach cafés serve chips with everything and there's a supply of Malta's excellent soft ice cream.

Across the road that curves round the bay are the wetlands of the **Għadira Nature Reserve**, which offers some measure of protection to birdlife from Malta's destructive hunters. The merciless killing by the Maltese of what little wildlife their country possesses has received scant attention from successive governments, fearful of forfeiting precious votes should they attempt to curb this unsavoury national pastime.

On the far side of the bay is the Mellieħa Bay Hotel, which enjoys one of the most striking seascapes on the island across the water to **Mellieħa** village, crowned by its parish **Church of Our Lady of Victory** high on the ridge. Down the hill a short way, a long flight of steps leads to the chapel of **Our Lady of the Grotto**, carved from the rock with a faded fresco of the Virgin Mary attributed to St Luke.

Mellieħa, balanced about its steeply sloping main street of shops and restaurants, is a bustling community of distinctive character. A self-styled rural hub, it has origins in the 15th century and was one of Malta's earliest parishes. Until the early 1990s, the village was regularly jam-packed with cars; now the bypass road with its breathtaking coastal panorama whisks traffic bound for Mellieħa Bay and Gozo well away from the built-up area.

Below: *The Knights' Red Tower fortification.*

From Mellieħa there is a fine vista of the rocky island of Comino, with Gozo's church-dominated skyline beyond. On the slopes around Mellieħa the grapes are grown for the islands' limited production of red and white wine.

Marfa Ridge ★★

The high ground beyond Mellieħa Bay belongs to the Marfa Ridge, protected by the 1649 **Red Tower** of the Knights. Driving along the narrow ridge road past the Red Tower to **Ras il-Qammieħ** there are stunning views across the Comino Channel to Gozo and Comino.

From a shrine at the crest of the hill, the narrow road on the right follows the ridge to the **Madonna statue** and a tiny **chapel** on a remote and windy part of the island favoured by the hunting fraternity.

All the side lanes from the ridge road head down across the rugged landscape to little bays beyond the ridge. These include **Ramla Bay**, **Armier Bay** with its collection of holiday homes and the attractive yet oddly named **Slug Bay**, situated below the **White Tower**. These bays attract many more Maltese than tourists, who tend to favour bigger stretches like Mellieħa Bay and Golden Bay. In winter, the extreme north of the island is deserted, its holiday homes barred and bolted – as such, it makes fine walking country.

A few hundred metres before reaching the Gozo ferry terminal of Ċirkewwa, a side road leads uphill to a small cliff-top car park overlooking **Paradise Bay**.

NORTHWEST MALTA

Overlooking the yellow sands of **Golden Bay** is the Radisson SAS Golden Sands Resort and Spa, an expansive five-star property that opened its doors in 2005. Around the flat-topped headland is **Għajn Tuffieħa Bay** (the name means 'eye of the

POPEYE VILLAGE

Whether or not you saw the 1980 film *Popeye*, the film set at **Anchor Bay** is a real treat. The 17 painted wooden water's-edge houses of tumble-down Sweethaven have been revived after threatening for years to collapse into the sea through neglect. The Paramount film by Robert Altman starred Robin Williams as Popeye and Shelley Duvall as Olive Oyl and is available on video. A cinema by the entrance shows a film about the making of Sweethaven. A horse-riding trail from stables near Golden Bay passes by Anchor Bay.

Below: *Painted wooden houses at Popeye Village.*

Below: *The golden sand of Għajn Tuffieħa Bay, one of Malta's prettiest beaches.*

apple'), prettier even than Golden Bay and reached by a long flight of steps. Both beaches can be reached by bus from Valletta and become crowded in summer, Golden Bay especially so. A good time to visit in high season is late afternoon, when the crowds start to thin out.

Generally quieter is the smaller **Ġnejna Bay** (it translates as 'small garden'), with a neat line of boathouses cut into the limestone cliff. The bay is signposted west of Mġarr through the green Ġnejna Valley, abundant with figs, vines and tall bamboo. **Mġarr** itself (like Żebbuġ and Rabat it has a twin of the same name in Gozo) has the large **Church of the Assumption**, which was funded by villagers through the sale of eggs – and in recognition the dome was given the appearance of an egg.

HISTORIC SITES

Northern Malta has some of the island's oldest archaeological remains – earlier even than the Ġgantija temples on Gozo. The **Skorba** site, just outside the village of Żebbiegħ, provided Malta with its earliest Neolithic ruins; evidence of two temples and several houses indicate this was a village of some size. Another prehistoric site on the edge of Mġarr is **Ta' Ħaġrat**, with what is left of two temples of the Skorba type believed to date from 3000–2500BC. Just outside the village stands a modern mansion, **Zammitello Palace**. Guarding the coastline are the **Għajn Znuber** watchtower at the western end of the Marfa Ridge, a tower between Golden and Għajn Tuffieħa bays and the **Lippia Tower** inland of Ġnejna Bay.

While it is known that Malta prospered under the Romans, little evidence of the period remains. Some villas have been excavated and in 1929 the **Roman baths** near Għajn Tuffieħa came to light. The site was restored with UNESCO money in the 1960s.

The North at a Glance

Summer is the most popular season for visiting Malta's north, with the beaches attracting thousands of visitors between June and September. Prospective winter vacationers should consider staying in Sliema or St Julian's, where there is much more going on out of season.

The north of Malta is best reached at the end of a scenic drive along the **coast road** from the Sliema/Valletta direction. Fine views of Gozo and Comino unfold the further north you go, along with some excellent panoramas of the rugged northwest coast.

There are fewer roads in Malta's northern reaches owing to the rugged nature of the landscape. The main **road** from St Paul's Bay passes Mellieħa Bay before climbing Marfa Ridge and dropping to the Gozo ferry point at Ċirkewwa. **Bus** services, most linking the resorts and bays of the north with Valletta, also offer good connections around the region.

Qawra/St Paul's Bay
Suncrest, Qawra Coast Road, tel: 2157 7101, fax: 2157 5478. Four-star hotel that dominates Qawra's seafront with a large waterside lido.

Grand Hotel Mercure San Antonio, St Paul's Bay, tel: 2158 3434, fax: 2157 2481. North African feel to this stylish four-star hotel of the French Accor group.
Dolmen Resort Hotel, Qawra, tel: 2355 2355, fax: 2355 5666. Large modern four-star built around Neolithic remains at the meeting of Buġibba and Qawra.

Mellieħa Area
Selmun Palace, Selmun, tel: 2152 1040, fax: 2152 1060. Hilltop location for this four-star popular with continental visitors.
Mellieħa Bay, tel: 2157 3841, fax: 2157 6399. Four-star favoured by the British, with splendid views across the bay and beach to Mellieħa village.
Maritim Antonine Hotel & Spa, Borg Olivier Street, Mellieħa, tel: 2152 0923, fax: 2152 0930. Modern four-star hotel with spa in Mellieħa village.

Bays to the North
Paradise Bay, tel: 2152 1166, fax: 2152 1153. Large four-star next to Gozo ferry terminal, Ċirkewwa.
Barceló Riviera, Marfa, tel: 2152 5900, fax: 2152 5142. Quiet four-star spa resort with diving centre facing Comino.
Ramla Bay, tel: 2281 2281, fax: 2281 2282. Remote north coast four-star at the end of a lane off Marfa Ridge facing Comino.

Savini, Qawra Road, tel: 2157 6927. Grand dining, upper-range Italian cuisine with excellent service.
Da Rosi, Church Street, St Paul's Bay, tel: 2157 1411. Friday is speciality fish night.
Gillieru, St Paul's Bay seafront, tel: 2157 3480. An inexpensive restaurant with a good reputation for fish.
Palazzo Santa Rosa, Mistra Bay, tel: 2158 2737. More expensive restaurant located in a converted seaside farmhouse.
Don Alfredo, Church Street, St Paul's Bay, tel: 2157 3759. Water's edge restaurant specializing in Mediterranean cuisine, fish and Maltese dishes.
L'Escargot, Borg Olivier Street, Mellieħa, tel: 2152 3553. Bistro at the top of the hill, good for light bites and Maltese fare.
The Arches, Main Street, Mellieħa, tel: 2152 3460. More expensive, but with reputation for top-class cuisine.

Captain Morgan Cruises, tel: 2346 3333, operates **boat trips** from Buġibba to Comino and around Gozo; they also operate an **Underwater Safari boat**. **Maltaqua**, tel: 2157 1873, 2157 2558, offers diving tuition, ranging from beginners to advanced level.

Tourist information, 1 City Gate, Valletta, tel: 2123 7747.

9
GOZO

Most visitors to Gozo are day-trippers, arriving by ferry in mid-morning and leaving in late afternoon. The little island welcomes 400,000 day visitors annually and local businesses thrive as a result. But to fully appreciate Gozo you need to stay for a bit longer, enjoy the relaxed lifestyle of this traditional farming and fishing community, and recognize the world of difference that exists between the island and its larger neighbour.

Gozo is just over a quarter the size of Malta – 15km (9½ miles) long by 7km (4½ miles) at its widest point – while its rocky shoreline of bays and inlets measures 43km (27 miles). Of the Maltese islands' total population of 350,000, some 26,000 live in Gozo. While Malta's people seem ever to be on the move, however, those in Gozo give the impression of having discovered the ultimate laid-back approach to life.

This is where the Maltese go when they want to get away from it all. Gozo is different enough to feel like another country, yet it is only a 20-minute ferry trip away. And though many Gozitans 'emigrate' to Malta, they remain first and foremost proudly Gozitans, faithful to the isle they call Għawdex (pronounced Ow-desh). This was an Arabic corruption of earlier names and has always been preferred by the locals to the Spanish version, Gozo, which was imposed upon them.

Thanks to its distinctive blue-clay soil, Gozo stays green even in high summer, when its neat, cultivated terraces contrast with Malta's sun-baked surfaces.

MEDITERRANEAN SEA

MEDITERRANEAN SEA

Opposite: *Rural Gozo looking from the Citadel.*

YEAR OF REVENGE

Gozo's blackest year was 1551, when **Dragut Rias** led a Turkish raid to exact revenge for the death of his brother, who seven years previously had been captured and killed on Gozo. The Turks invaded the island, killing or carrying off into slavery almost the entire population of 5000. Fourteen years later, Dragut himself perished during the Great Siege of Malta.

The Gozitans have long been farmers and part-time fishermen – today the smaller island provides Malta with much of its produce, hand-tilled in tiny fields and often transported by donkey cart. Villages crown the hilltops, both as a measure of defence and to leave the valley floors free for crops; in spring the countryside bursts forth in a profusion of wild flowers.

The proximity of the two islands means that Gozo's history and culture have been inextricably linked to those of Malta, though both were self-governing from the Roman period until the arrival of the Knights. In modern times, Gozo has again established some autonomy, albeit limited. The island was given its own government ministry in 1987 and it has achieved a good deal. Compared to its larger neighbour, the roads are better, the capital and villages are cleaner and tidier and there is generally a stronger environmental awareness.

The Maltese government is trying to establish Gozo as an upmarket holiday spot and has encouraged the development of top-quality hotels such as L'Imġarr and the Kempinski San Lawrenz. The government is aware, however, that over-development could easily destroy Gozo's appeal and has restricted the building of new holiday accommodation to deluxe standard. In keeping with this upmarket image, there are converted farmhouses and modern apartments with their own swimming pools.

Below: *Country transport: the donkey cart is still widely used in Gozo's rural areas.*

VICTORIA

Gozo's chief town and traditional capital begs comparison with Mdina – a hilltop citadel rising proudly above the landscape, its sheer curtain walls visible from afar. Within the ramparts, a maze of alleyways disorientates the visitor; at the foot of the walls a wider mesh of side streets makes up Gozo's social and commercial hub. The city, formerly **Rabat**, was renamed Victoria in 1897 to celebrate Queen Victoria's diamond jubilee – a move not welcomed by the locals, who still refer to Rabat (meaning 'suburb') rather than Victoria, which can cause some confusion with the Rabat in Malta.

All the island's main roads radiate from the capital and you will need a good map to find your way around the island on the minor roads. However, Victoria is a place to visit rather than to stay in, as there are no hotels and few restaurants.

The Citadel ★★★

Gozo suffered severely at the hands of the Turks and other marauding raiders throughout the Middle Ages and the only solution appeared to be the construction of a city stronghold in which the population could gather in times of danger. The mighty bastions you see today, built around 1600 and funded jointly by King Philip II of Spain and the Gozitans themselves, were never put to the test.

Above: *The cathedral and remains of medieval houses within the Citadel, whose walls were built nearly 400 years ago as a refuge against the Turks.*

By that time the Turks had fled back east, leaving the Gozitans in relative peace – though spasmodic raids occurred into the 18th century.

In 1637 a law requiring all islanders to sleep within the Citadel was rescinded; the people moved out and thus began the decline of the old city's importance. Many of the vacated buildings within those walls were destroyed by the 1693 earthquake. Today the towering ramparts embrace the cathedral, a number of museums, some craft shops and crumbled medieval dwellings that were the subject of a restoration programme. Don't leave the Citadel without walking round the ramparts – the 360-degree panorama that unfolds offers the best views of Gozo.

INTO THE BREACH

Having stood firm for more than 300 years, the Citadel's curtain walls were finally breached in 1956 – not by an act of war but by workmen providing a grander entrance and exit for the feast day procession of Santa Maria on 15 August. Much criticized at the time, the new opening nevertheless created a grander view of the cathedral and the apron of steps leading up to it. The former main gateway is at the end of the approach road to the right of the breach.

The Cathedral ★★

From the outside it lacks the ornamentation of other prominent Maltese churches; on the inside the creation of Maltese architect **Lorenzo Gafa** is far from plain. The cathedral was started in 1697, replacing a previous church on the site, and completed in 1711. Once inside look skywards for the interior's focal point, the beautifully proportioned painting of the 1730s by Italian artist **Antonio Manuele** – a *trompe l'oeil* which gives the illusion of a vast dome. The cathedral roof is actually flat, funds having run short before its completion.

The Museums ★★

Victoria's Citadel, a historical treasure in itself, includes several small museums dedicated to Gozo. The **Archaeological Museum** in the 17th-century Palazzo Bondi, former home of an endowed Gozo family, contains excavated relics of the Ġgantija temples and includes a stone phallic symbol; there is also a model of the temple site, along with Roman amphorae (wine jars) and other finds.

In the vestry behind the cathedral, the **Cathedral Museum** has a collection of vestments, ceremonial pieces, manuscripts and portraits. There is also a ceremonial landau from around 1860 used by the Bishop of Gozo. The **Folklore Museum** recounts Gozo life down the years in displays occupying three medieval houses; crafts are shown here and also in the **Crafts Centre**, where products are displayed but are not for sale – business cards of the makers are alongside.

The **Natural Science Museum**, in a former storeroom of the Knights, identifies Gozo's flora and fauna and has a section on the marine environment. The Old Prison, overlooking Cathedral Square, was in use from the mid-16th century until the early 1900s and houses an exhibition on Gozo's fortifications.

The Main Square (It-Tokk) ★★

While the Citadel on its bluff first catches the eye, the real heart of Victoria is its main square, **Pjazza Independenza** – better known by its old name of **It-Tokk**, meaning 'meeting place'. The small, tree-lined square at the top of Republic Street is fringed with tiny shops and bars and has a daily morning market selling fruit, vegetables and local craftware. In the centre of the square is a statue of Christ that commemorates the fallen of World

Below: *Stepped alleyway in Victoria's Citadel, part of a maze of passages within the fortified walls.*

GETTING TO GOZO

• **Ferries** of the Gozo Channel Company run between Ċirkewwa in Malta and Mġarr in Gozo and operate more or less hourly round the clock in summer and from early until late in winter. Crossing with a car is both efficient and inexpensive. The crossing takes approximately 20 minutes.
• Thankfully, Gozo is still spared the noise and environmental pollution of its own airport. For visitors seeking a faster alternative to the ferries, a small heliport near Xewkija handles the **helicopter** link with Malta International Airport.

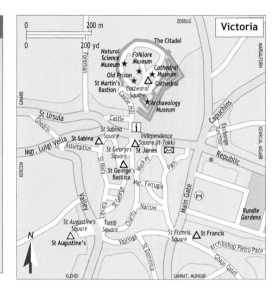

Victoria

Below: Xagħra's Ta-Kola windmill, a well-preserved example of the strong rural heritage of Gozo.

War II; on the edge the newly renovated **Church of St James**, from 1740, and the semi-circular **Banca Giuratale** built by Grand Master Manoel de Vilhena in 1733 to house the council of Gozo. It is now the site of local government offices.

St George's Basilica ★★

Behind It-Tokk, in the Pjazza San Gorg among the balconied streets of the old town, is the Baroque St George's Basilica, traditionally Gozo's first parish church. It was built in the 1670s and has been beautified over the years; fine artistic works inside include Mattia Preti's painting of St George with his foot victoriously placed on the head of the dragon. The bronze altar canopy is styled on one by Bernini in St Peter's in Rome.

Northern Gozo

Gozo's northern region is characterized by the green sweep of the long Marsalforn Valley, flanked by the two hilltop villages of Żebbuġ and Xagħra and ending in the attractive little seaside resort of Marsalforn. The bluff supporting Victoria's Citadel rises high above the head of the valley, which extends for some 3km (2 miles) towards the sea and is a picture of wild flowers in spring and early summer. There is a good road from Victoria to Marsalforn and also out to Żebbuġ and Xagħra; narrow lanes descend from the hilltop villages to the coast. A statue of Christ the Saviour stands atop a conical hill above the Marsalforn Valley.

Above: *Wild spring flowers bloom in the Marsalforn Valley.*

Xagħra ★

Crowned by its mighty 19th-century **Church of Our Lady of Victories** fronting the wide village square, Xagħra (pronounced Shar-ra) dominates Gozo's northern landscape; the village is one of Gozo's few growth areas and could soon rival Victoria for size. Just off the square is the distinctive and well-restored **Ta-Kola windmill** of 1725, one of several that once dotted the island, and now a small rural museum. Also in Xagħra is the Edward Lear-inspired **Pomskizillious Toy Museum** at 10 Ġnien Xibla Street, which includes exhibits more than 160 years old.

Two limestone caves discovered below houses in the village – **Ninu's Cave** (in 1888) and the larger **Xerri's Grotto** (in 1923) – have fascinating examples of stalactites and stalagmites. The owners will lead you down and point out the unusual geological forms created over the millennia.

CALYPSO'S ISLE

Local legend – and the Greek scholar Callimachus in the 3rd century BC – holds that Gozo is **Ogygia**, isle of the sea goddess Calypso in Homer's *Odyssey*. Calypso is said to have lured the Greek hero Odysseus on to the island as he returned from Troy and held him captive for seven years in the cave high above Ramla Bay before being ordered by Zeus to release him. The view across the golden beach of Ramla Bay is more impressive than Calypso's Cave, which despite its alluring name is just a narrow opening at the top of the rocky cliff.

Right: *The ancient structures at Ġgantija, most impressive of Malta and Gozo's temple sites.*

Ġgantija Temples ★★★

The largest and best preserved of the islands' prehistoric temple sites, Ġgantija is claimed to be the world's oldest free-standing structure – older even than the Egyptian pyramids and Stonehenge in Britain. According to legend, the massive blocks of Ġgantija (the word means 'gigantic') were carried from Ta' Ċenċ in the south of the island by a female giant between 3600 and 3000BC – some are as much as 6m (20ft) high and weigh many tonnes.

The complex, on a fenced-in hilltop site a few minutes' walk from the centre of Xagħra, was unearthed in 1827 and comprises two temples, built several centuries apart, with a forecourt. Each temple has five lobe-shaped apses leading off a central corridor; features within are the floor libation holes, limestone blocks with spiral decoration, an oracle hole and a stone recess for washing feet. The large altar blocks were almost certainly used for the sacrifice of animals.

Below: *The Knights' salt pans at Qbajjar.*

Nearby is the **Brochtorff Circle** underground cave complex with stone walls and arches that Gozo's inhabitants used for burials between 4000 and 2500 BC. The site, excavated since 1987, has yielded some fine figurines and skeletal remains.

Marsalforn **

Long a quiet fishing village, today Marsalforn is Gozo's chief holiday resort. It is still small and the setting attractive, with bars and restaurants aplenty around the bay and an array of souvenir shops where, if you are lucky, you may find the home-knitted woollens for which Gozo has a high reputation.

The whole seafront area has been enhanced in recent years, with better paving along the promenade and the short sand and shingle beach improved. A short distance to the west, at the foot of the narrow road from Żebbuġ, are the bays of **Xwieni** and **Qbajjar**, both good for swimming. From **Żebbuġ** itself, which is stretched out along the top of the ridge north of Victoria, there are superb views towards Marsalforn and west across the Għasri Valley, where a little sea inlet offers some good bathing.

Above: *Gozo's chief resort, Marsalforn, was once a small fishing village.*

Ramla Bay **

This is Gozo's one real sandy beach, with sand as golden as you will find anywhere and the water inviting, though care must be exercised because of currents. The beach is generally less crowded than those in Malta, even on the hottest days. This was a favoured landing place for invaders in the Middle Ages, prompting the Knights to construct an underwater defensive wall across the bay's

> **THE SALT PANS**
>
> Around the headland west of Marsalforn, at **Qbajjar**, the salt pans date back 250 years to the latter days of the Knights and are still very much in use. Locals harvest the white salt crust left by evaporated seawater in the rectangular rock-cut chambers, gathering several tonnes each year.

Above: *The limestone Azure Window near Dwejra Point.*
Opposite: *The national shrine of Ta' Pinu Basilica.*
Below: *Dwejra's cliffs aglow at sunset.*

entrance, the remains of which can still be seen. To the west, near the top of the cliff, is the legendary **Calypso's Cave**; inland among the dunes is the site of a **Roman villa**.

WESTERN GOZO

The barren landscape that falls away from San Lawrenz towards the sea near Gozo's westernmost point has a fascination bred by the feeling that you might just have reached the ends of the earth. This bleached coastline of cliffs and caves strikes a pleasing contrast with the deep blue Mediterranean and erosion has created a fine natural arch, the **Azure Window** or *Tieqa Zerqa*. Tread lightly across this bridge of fossilized seashells – its collapse has been predicted for years.

A short way offshore in Dwejra Bay is the sheer-sided **Fungus Rock** (also *Il-Ġebla tal-Ġeneral* or General's Rock), whose unusual vegetation cover was highly prized by the Knights as a cure for dysentery and haemorrhaging. The only access was by rope and pulley from the Qawra Tower on the shore; anyone found attempting to steal the red 'fungus' was put to death.

The third feature of geological interest is the **Inland Sea**, a sheltered seawater pool flanked by high cliffs and linked by a natural passageway to the open sea. Small boats leave here for trips through the tunnel and along the coast; a little rustic bar among the boathouses provides welcome refreshment.

Ta' Pinu Basilica ★★

Alone in the fields between Għarb and Għammar stands Malta's national shrine of Ta' Pinu, a Romanesque centre of pilgrimage that was given basilica status in 1932. Passing a small 16th-century chapel here in 1883, local spinster Carmel Grima heard a voice telling her to pray; a friend, Francesco Portelli, affirmed that he had also heard the voice. They prayed together for his sick mother, who made an unexpected recovery.

Miracle cures followed in the area and from thanksgiving offerings the present sanctuary was built in the 1920s; it incorporates the original chapel, whose early caretaker Pinu Gauci lent his name to the site.

The Villages

Of Gozo's smaller villages, **Għarb** is among the prettiest. Its ornate and balconied houses cluster around the 17th-century Baroque Parish Church of the Immaculate Conception with its unusual concave façade and sculptures of Faith, Hope and Charity. The **Għarb Folklore Museum**, in an 18th-century village house, highlights Maltese and Gozitan traditions.

Within a kilometre of Għarb are the hamlets of **Birbuba**, **Għammar** and **Santa Pietru**. At the top of the road leading downwards to Dwejra Point is **San Lawrenz**; to the right of the road which heads back towards Victoria is the **Ta' Dbiegi Craft Village**, where you can see lacemaking and weaving and watch pottery, ceramics and glass being made. It is open year round.

> ### GOZO LACE
>
> The ladies of Gozo have a well-earned reputation as being among the world's best lacemakers. The craft was introduced from Genoa in 1846 in an effort to raise the standard of living of the poorest islanders and developed into a fully fledged industry, supporting tourism and providing Gozo with its best-known souvenirs. The lace, called *bacilli*, is made to a stencilled design on a lacemaker's pillow by using bobbins; the finished articles – tablecloths, handkerchiefs, mats, table napkins, doilies and bookmarks – are extremely good value.

THE NUNS' STEPS

To the right of the bay as you face the sea at Xlendi, there is a flight of steps cut into the rock. Climb them for an excellent view of Xlendi's tiny waterfront and then descend to **Caroline's Cave**, a small natural cove named after a wealthy spinster who in 1889 founded a group of nursing nuns, the Dominican Sisters of Malta. She paid for these steps to be cut so the nuns could enjoy private bathing – the gate the sisters locked behind them remains today.

SOUTHERN GOZO

The wild cliffs of southern Gozo are the highest on the island, rising nearly 150m (500ft) either side of Xlendi Bay. The compact resort of Xlendi sits at the seaward end of a 3km (2 mile) valley leading southwest from Victoria; halfway down, a side road heads eastwards across the valley to Munxar. Occupying two hills either side of the Hanzira Valley beyond Munxar are the villages of Xewkija and Sannat.

Xlendi ★★

The scenic road to Xlendi descends quickly from Victoria and runs down a steep-sided valley with views across to Munxar. On the way it passes the 17th-century **Knights' Wash House** in Victoria's 'suburb' village of Fontana, built by the order over a spring that supplied the locals with water.

A delightful little seaside village, Xlendi has maintained its appeal as Gozo's second resort to Marsalforn despite living in the shadow of a massive bank of tourist apartments. On the tiny promenade, a handful of open-air cafés and souvenir shops vie for business either side of the St Patrick's Hotel. In summer, small boats bob in front of the narrow sandy beach, sheltered by tall cliffs and guarded by the Xlendi Tower, one of many such defences ringing the Maltese islands and built in 1658.

Below: *Tiny Xlendi at the head of its landlocked bay. The calm water in the bay is ideal for swimming.*

Sannat ★

The small village of Sannat is known for its lacemaking and for one of the really outstanding hotels in the Maltese islands, Ta' Ċenċ. The hotel, which blends inconspicuously with its extensive grounds, takes its name from the cliffs to the south, the highest on Gozo and nesting site for a variety of bird life. Near the hotel, ancient burial mounds, a dolmen and cart ruts of the kind found on Malta (*see* p. 94) are evidence that the area was occupied in prehistoric times. Sannat's **Parish Church of St Margaret** was built in 1718 on the site formerly occupied by a smaller church.

Between Sannat and Xewkija, a narrow lane leads down through the steep-sided Ħanzira Valley to the attractive narrow inlet of **Mġarr ix-Xini**, a quiet spot which is good for bathing. The short walk from Ta' Ċenċ leads across open countryside, with excellent views to the west of the sheer cliffs so closely identified with this part of the island.

Xewkija ★

Dominating the skyline of the area, and indeed that of the whole of Gozo, is Xewkija's mighty **Rotunda**, or dome, the fourth largest in Europe and only just beaten into third place by the Mosta Dome on Malta.

Above left: *Ideal for relaxation: the cafés along the promenade at Xlendi.*
Above right: *Lacemaking on Gozo, the island's most famous home industry.*

XEWKIJA'S ROTUNDA

The church in Xewkija which incorporates the famous Rotunda is dedicated to St John the Baptist. It was financed by parishioners and built by local labour between 1952 and 1971 on the site of a small 17th-century Baroque church. A measure of its vast size is that Xewkija's entire population of more than 3000 would only make for a medium-sized congregation.
The Rotunda has been compared in style and proportion to Santa Maria della Salute in Venice.

Above: *The harbour of Mġarr, entry port to Gozo. Above the harbour is Fort Chambrai, built in the 18th century by the Knights.*

NO FAT CATS HERE!

Don't feel pity for the thin cats you see on your travels in Malta. All Maltese cats are naturally slimline and are equipped to cope with the hot summer weather – they are not necessarily in need of a good meal. Many live wild and enjoy very different lives to their north European cousins, with hand-outs from benevolent hoteliers and fishermen taking the place of canned cat food. Whole families of cats can be seen living together in relative harmony. Note also the long pointed face characteristic of the Maltese cat.

EASTERN GOZO
Mġarr ★★

Although Mġarr is the main port of entry from Malta, many visitors pass straight through towards Victoria and then the resorts of Marsalforn and Xlendi. In fact Eastern Gozo is the most peaceful and rural part of the island and Mġarr itself remains a favourite subject of Maltese watercolour artists. The view from the ferry is of a busy little harbour packed with *luzzu* boats, yachts and ferries, and a skyline pierced by the spires of two churches. The graceful 19th-century Gothic-style **Our Lady of Lourdes** is nowadays dwarfed by the much larger church of Għajnsielem, the neighbouring village on the road to Victoria.

High to the left are the ramparts of **Fort Chambrai**, ambitiously planned as a fortress town in the early 1700s by Grand Master Manoel de Vilhena but never completed as such. The fortifications of the Knights' last major defensive work were eventually finished thanks to the private funding of the Order's French admiral Jacques François de Chambray. When the French invaded in 1798 it was the only fortification to put up any resistance; later it served as a British garrison, a place of convalescence for Allies wounded at Gallipoli in 1915, a mental hospital, a low-grade tourist complex and as government housing. The latest of many plans call for it to be turned into a high-class, 250-bed holiday village. On the opposite side of the harbour, offering guests exceptional views across the Comino Channel to Comino and Malta, is the five-star **L'Imġarr Hotel**.

Nadur ★

On a hill north of Mġarr, 150m (500ft) above sea level, is the large and prosperous village of Nadur – in Arabic the name means 'summit' – from where vigilant locals kept watch for unwanted visitors in the time of the Knights. The splendid **Parish Church of St Peter and St Paul** was designed in the 18th century by Maltese architect Giuseppe Bonici and contains some fine stained glass.

On the edge of nearby Qala is a distinctive Gozo windmill of the 19th century, which was in use until the 1980s. The small village also has the 17th-century **Sanctuary of the Immaculate Conception**, on the site of an 11th-century chapel, and the square-towered **Church of Santa Marija** with its neat churchyard overlooking the sea.

Beyond Nadur and Qala there are the small but exquisite beaches of San Blas and Hondoq bays.

SAN BLAS BAY

● One of the most scenically attractive little beaches of the Maltese islands is at **San Blas Bay**. Follow the sign to the bay out of Nadur and take the single-track road downwards – above the bay there is parking space for three cars at a squeeze. A surfaced footpath leads steeply down past culti-vated terraces to the tiny sandy bay. It is one of the truly peaceful spots on the planet.
● Another small beach at the eastern end of the island is at **Hondoq Bay**. The road east from Qala winds down to the usually deserted sandy inlet, where the water takes on a brilliant turquoise appearance to rival that of Comino's famed Blue Lagoon.

Below: *San Blas Bay, one of Gozo's best-kept secrets.*

Žebbuġ
Xagħra
Gozo
Victoria
Mġarr
Comino
Mellieħa
Malta
MEDITERRANEAN SEA

Below: *The Comino Tower, guarding the channel between Malta and Gozo.*

COMINO

In mid-channel between Malta and Gozo sits the island of Comino, all 2.5 km² (1 sq mile) of it, which can be reached from both Malta and Gozo. Historically a pirates' haven, Comino is today the refuge of tourists seeking solitude, relaxation and every water sport under the furnace-like summer sun.

There are no cars or roads on Comino; a short coastal path links the island's low-rise four-star tourist accommodation, the Comino Hotel and Comino Suites, in adjacent bays.

From the Gozo ferry you can make out the sparkling turquoise waters of the **Blue Lagoon** on the fractured coast between Comino and the islet of Cominotto. From mid-morning to early afternoon it usually has a full complement of tourist boats and it is a favourite haunt of scuba divers, who have plenty to explore in a fascinating underwater world of caves and grottos.

The island's dominant feature is the **Comino Tower**, built in 1618 by Grand Master Alof de Wignacourt to protect the Comino Channel from raiders and later used as a hunting lodge. There are also the remains of a former isolation hospital used by the British in World War I, the small Gothic **St Mary's Chapel** dating from the late 1600s in which masses are still held, possibly the world's smallest police station and a pig farm. A handful of people live on the island year-round.

Gozo at a Glance

Malta's sister islands of Gozo and Comino are best enjoyed in **springtime**, when visitors can enjoy their fine rural aspects and admire Gozo's profusion of wild flowers.

The Gozo Channel Company operates a year-round **car ferry** service from Cirkewwa on Malta's north-western tip (see Travel Tips on p. 125 for details.)

Finding your way around Gozo is easy, as nearly all roads radiate from the capital Victoria. **Car hire** is available in Gozo from Victor J. Borg Enterprises, tel: 2155 1866. Bus services radiate from the bus station in Victoria. Service **25** runs between the Mġarr ferry point and Victoria, from where you can reach Marsalforn (service 21), Xlendi (service 87) and other villages on the island. **Taxis** are available, but at a cost. A **motor launch** runs in summer from Mġarr to Comino; there is also a boat link from Mtarfa in Malta.

Northern Gozo
Cornucopia, Ġnien Imrik Street, tel: 2155 6486, fax: 2155 2910. Superb four-star farmhouse conversion at Xagħra with great pool area.
Calypso, Marsalforn Bay,

tel: 2156 2000, fax: 2156 2012. Four-star hotel in great quayside setting.

Southern Gozo
Ta' Ċenċ, Cenc Street, Sannat, tel: 2155 6819, fax: 2155 8199. Outstanding five-star hotel with bungalow-style rooms in extensive grounds.
St Patrick's, Xlendi Promenade, tel: 2156 2951, fax: 2155 6598. Comfortable four-star hotel at water's edge.
San Andrea, Xlendi Promenade, tel: 2156 5555, fax: 2156 5400. Nice three-star by the bay.

Eastern Gozo
L'Imġarr, tel: 2156 0455, fax: 2155 7589. Five-star clifftop hotel above Mġarr harbour.

Comino
Comino, tel: 2152 9821, fax: 2152 9826. Hotel and suites in adjacent bays provide the only accommodation on tiny Comino.

Cornucopia Hotel, Gnien Imrik Street, Xagħra, tel: 2155 6486. Great lunchtime pasta, good evening selection.
Vinyard, Mġarr Road, Victoria, tel: 2155 9976. Large medium-priced menu in renovated surroundings.
Jeffreys, Għarb Road, Għarb, tel: 2156 1006. Splendid value, handwritten menu which changes daily; rural ambience. May be closed in winter.
Il-Kenur, Victoria Road,

Xlendi, tel: 2551 1583. Serves a good mid-priced selection. Also has a fixed-price menu.
Oleander, Victory Square, Xagħra, tel: 2155 7230. Great value, authentic Gozitan meals served overlooking the square.
Stone Crab, Xlendi Bay, tel: 2155 6400. Whole lamb stuffed with spinach and mozzarella at the water's edge.

Full-day **excursions** operate to Gozo from the resorts on Malta. **Jeep safaris** go off the beaten track to see parts of the island not seen on regular coach tours. **Evening trips** to Gozo take in the sunset at Dwejra. The principal operators are Josephine's, tel: 2131 0435; and Nova Tours, tel: 2157 5240, 2157 5960.
Boat trips from Sliema and Buġibba visit Comino: Captain Morgan, tel: 2346 3333, is the chief operator.
Dive specialists offering tuition include: Calypso Diving Centre, tel: 2156 1757; Nautic Team, tel: 2155 8507; and St Andrew's Divers Cove, tel: 2155 1301.

Tourist Information, Tigrija Palazz, Victoria, tel: 2156 1419.
Gozo Heritage, tel: 2156 1280.
Police, tel: 191.
Gozo General Hospital, tel: 2156 1600.

Travel Tips

Tourist Information

Malta National Tourist Offices abroad include Australia (Sydney), Austria (Vienna), Belgium (Brussels), France (Paris), Germany (Frankfurt), Holland (Amsterdam), Ireland (Dublin), Israel (Tel Aviv), Italy (Milan), Japan (Tokyo), Kuwait, Russia (Moscow), Sweden (Stockholm), Switzerland (Zürich), the United Kingdom (London) and the USA (New York).

The Malta Tourism Authority is at Auberge d'Italie, Merchants Street, Valletta CMR 02, tel: 2291 5000, fax: 2291 5394. Tourist Information Offices within Malta can be found at Malta International Airport (arrivals lounge), tel: 2369 6073; 1 City Gate, Valletta, tel: 2123 7747; Spinola Palace, St Julian's, tel: 2316 0420; and Tigrija Palazz, Victoria, Gozo, tel: 2156 1419.

Entry Requirements

Nationals of most countries, including the United Kingdom, may enter Malta for up to three months on production of a valid passport. A visa is required in a few cases.

Customs

Duty-free allowances are 200 cigarettes (or 50 cigars, 100 cigarillos or 250g of tobacco), one litre bottle of spirits and one litre bottle of wine, 60ml of perfume and 250ml of eau de toilette; and gifts to a value not exceeding Lm 50. From EU countries the limits are 800 cigarettes (or 200 cigars, 400 cigarillos or 1kg of tobacco), 10 litres of spirits, 20 litres of fortified wine, 90 litres of wine, 10 litres of beer and gifts up to Lm 50. There are duty-free shops in the arrival and departure halls at Malta International Airport.

Health Requirements

No health precautions are needed by visitors to Malta. A yellow fever immunization certificate is required from travellers arriving from an infected area.

Getting to Malta

By air: The national airline Air Malta operates direct scheduled services to Malta International Airport from points throughout Europe, the Middle East and North Africa; from the UK, British Airways

and Ryanair also operate. Malta is also served by airlines of many other European countries. It is also possible to book seats on charter flights operating to Malta – contact your travel agent. Flight inquiries, tel: 5004 3333; general inquiries, tel: 2124 9600 or 2169 7800.

By sea: The high-speed catamaran services of Virtu Ferries, tel: 2122 8777, operate from Pozzallo and Catania in Sicily to Malta. The Gozo Channel Company, tel: 2155 6114, operates the inter-island service between Malta and Gozo.

What to Pack

In summer the minimum is required – lightweight casual clothing which can be easily washed suffices and you don't need to take pullovers, cardigans or jackets as it stays warm until late evening. If you burn easily, take something to cover the shoulders and arms as Malta's sun can be intense. Children should wear a T-shirt over their swimwear in the pool or sea to prevent burning. If you feel like glamming up in the evening, you won't feel out of place as the Maltese tend to dress up rather than down when they go out. In winter, although temperatures might look good, warm clothing is necessary as the air can be damper than expected and the stone buildings can be cold.

Money Matters

Currency: When the Maltese decided to dispense with the pound as a unit of currency – it was seen as a relic of British rule – the way was clear to introduce a fresh name for its money. However, it opted for the lira (Lm), which can cause confusion with the Turkish lira. To complicate matters further, some shops still use the £ sign and most shopkeepers refer to Malta pounds rather than liri (the plural of lira). There are 100 cents to the lira. Notes are Lm 2, Lm 5, Lm 10 and Lm 20; coins are Lm 1 and 1, 2, 5, 10, 25 and 50 cents. As a new member of the European Union, Malta is due to switch to the Euro as a unit of currency, probably in 2008.

Exchange: Malta's two main banks are the Bank of Valletta (BOV) and HSBC; both have branches throughout the island with currency exchange facilities. There is a 24-hour exchange facility at Malta International Airport. Other banks are Lombard Bank and APS Bank. Smaller bureaux de change are found in Valletta and tourist areas. The maximum sum in local currency allowed into the country is Lm 1000 per person; the limit on departure is the same. To change Maltese currency back it is necessary to present exchange receipts.

Banks are usually open between 08:30 and 12:30 Mon–Fri, and until 11:30 on Sat. Some banks are open for longer and summer/winter opening hours may differ. ATMs are available for cash withdrawals throughout the main tourist areas.

Credit cards: International credit cards are widely accepted in hotels, restaurants and most shops. Expect to use cash in smaller shops, bars and snack bars.

Tipping: Taxi drivers 10%; restaurants 10%, unless a service charge has been added to the bill; porters 20c per piece of luggage.

Taxes: Prices displayed include VAT; the standard rate is 18%, with a reduced rate of 5% on some products and services. Food, pharmaceutical products and transport are exempt.

Accommodation

Malta has hotels and self-catering properties to suit every pocket, from deluxe hotels to no-frills guesthouses, and luxury villas or converted farmhouses to basic apartments. Hotels are graded from one to five stars and tourist villages and guesthouses from first to third class. Aparthotels, offering apartment-style accommodation with full hotel facilities, can also be found. There are

no official camping or caravan sites in the islands.

Eating Out

This is simply no problem. Eat cheaply or expensively according to your pocket, your mood and your taste – from a simple bowl of pasta in the sun to something far more formal with several courses that demands collar and tie. Malta's resort areas of Sliema, St Paul's Bay and St Julian's have a high concentration of places to eat out and other restaurants are scattered throughout the islands. For the widest choice of restaurants head for the St Julian's area – here there are also a large number of discos and music bars that will appeal to younger visitors. The capital Valletta has few restaurants; a much wider choice is available in nearby Sliema. Options include Indian, Chinese, Far East, Italian and Turkish, besides traditional Maltese, pizzerias and pasta-houses aplenty. You can also dine well in hotel restaurants, many of which serve a traditional Sunday lunch.

Transport

Though substantial investment in Malta's road system in recent years has improved internal communications, journey times are generally slow and the Valletta–Sliema– St Julian's conurbation, Ħamrun and Birkirkara can be especially busy. The underground multistorey car park for 1800 cars outside Valletta's City Gate is handy for the capital as parking within Valletta is severely restricted by the narrowness of the roads.

While road signposting has been improved, you will probably still find yourself navigating by the sun in remoter country areas where signs are occasional or non-existent. In Gozo this is less of a problem – most roads radiate from the island's capital Victoria.

Road: Car hire in Malta is among the cheapest in the Mediterranean; rates are fully inclusive and the daily rate usually works out cheaper if the car is hired for a week or longer. Even hiring a car at Malta Airport can pay for three days rental by saving a Lm 10 taxi fare each way.

All valid national driving licences and international driving licences are recognized. While Maltese law allows driving from 18 years with no upper age limit, some companies restrict car hire to those over 25 and under 70. International car rental companies such as Avis, Hertz, Budget and Europcar operate alongside local companies, of which Wembleys is one of the largest. If you are involved in an accident, call the police; do not move the car before the police have made their on-the-spot report, or it may invalidate your insurance.

Road rules: Driving is on the left in Malta, a legacy of British rule; the speed limit is 40kph (25mph) in built-up areas and 64kph (40mph) elsewhere. Road signs are international; traffic lights have been installed throughout the island in the last few years. Petrol stations are open Monday–Saturday from 07:00–19:00 in summer; 07:00–18:00 in winter. A few garages open on a rota until midday on Sundays and public holidays; outside those hours self-service is often available.

Taxis: Travelling by taxi is not cheap and fares increase sharply after midnight. Taxis are white (often Mercedes), with distinctive red number plates and are metered to display government-controlled prices, though the meter is not always switched on – if this is the case, make sure you agree the fare in advance. Taxis are readily available at the airport and on ranks in the main resort areas; some larger hotels

CONVERSION CHART

FROM	TO	MULTIPLY BY
Millimetres	inches	0·0394
Metres	yards	1·0936
Metres	feet	3·281
Kilometres	miles	0·6214
Square kilometres	square miles	0.386
Hectares	acres	2·471
Litres	pints	1·760
Kilograms	pounds	2·205
Tonnes	tons	0·984

To convert Celsius to Fahrenheit: x 9 ÷ 5 + 32

have their own rank. Note that Maltese taxis do not cruise the streets in the hope of picking up a fare. It is possible to hire a taxi for a day's sightseeing, but again agree the price first.

Buses: A ride on one of Malta's old bone-shaker buses should not be missed. Many of them were introduced back in the 1950s after conversion from vehicles of the British armed forces and are now tourist attractions in themselves. They were formerly colour-coded to differentiate between destinations, but are now uniformly yellow with an orange band. There are more than 500 buses in Malta, many owned by the drivers. Public transport in Malta operates frequently and is amazingly cheap, with fares from 20 cents (on certain routes between main resort areas the cost of a ride can be more). Routes radiate from the Valletta bus terminus outside City Gate to every town, village and sandy beach in the island. You might save on the cost of travel by buying a one-day (Lm 1.50), three-day (Lm 4), five-day (Lm 5) or weekly (Lm 6) ticket. In Gozo, buses (grey with a red stripe) serve the main villages from Victoria but run only infrequently.

Ferry: A ferry service operates half-hourly from the Strand in Sliema (the area is still referred to as the Ferries from the steam ferries

PUBLIC HOLIDAYS

Malta observes the following public holidays:

1 January • New Year's Day
10 February • St Paul's Shipwreck
19 March • St Joseph
31 March • Freedom Day
Good Friday (variable)
1 May • Workers' Day
7 June • 'Sette Giugno'
29 June • St Peter and St Paul
15 August • The Assumption
8 September • Our Lady of Victories
21 September • Independence Day
8 December • The Immaculate Conception
13 December • Republic Day
25 December • Christmas Day

of old) across Marsamxett Harbour to Valletta. It is a good alternative to the road trip – and quicker, too. Departure times are advertised at the Sliema departure point.

The **Gozo ferry** service is operated by The Gozo Channel Company. The 6km (4-mile) crossing from Ċirkewwa in northwest Malta to Mġarr in Gozo takes about 20 minutes. The car-carrying service operates every 45 minutes in summer (every hour and a half at night); the frequency changes from late September to late June. Winter cross-

ings can be affected by weather conditions – if in doubt, check with the Gozo Channel Company, tel: 2155 6114. Return fares are Lm 6.75 for a car and driver, Lm 2 per adult and 50c per child, confusingly paid at a kiosk on the Gozo side before the return journey.

Business hours

Offices: Offices in Malta and Gozo switch over to summer working hours for July, August and September – generally 07:30–13:30. For the rest of the year, working hours are 08:30–17:00 with a break for lunch.

Shops: Shops open from 09:00–13:00 and again from 16:00–19:00 on Monday–Saturday; they are closed on Sunday and public holidays (see panel). Many shops in tourist areas stay open throughout the day.

Time

Malta is on Central European Time, one hour ahead of Greenwich Mean (Universal Standard) Time in winter and two hours ahead of GMT from the last Sunday in March to the last Sunday in September. The islands are six hours ahead of the USA's Eastern Standard Winter Time and seven hours ahead in summer.

Communications

Big investment in Malta's telephone system has worked wonders in recent years, for making both international and local calls. Telephone numbers in Malta and Gozo are eight-figure numbers, usually starting with '21', and there is no area code. To call Malta from abroad, dial the international access code followed by 356. For local inquiries in Malta as well as in Gozo, dial 190, and for international (overseas) inquiries, dial 194.

STD dialling is available to most countries, including the UK (code 0044), USA and Canada (001), South Africa (0027) and Australia (0061). There are **post offices** in most towns and villages; hours are usually 07:30– 12:45 but can vary. The post office in Valletta at Dar L-Annona, Castille Place, is open from 08:15–16:30 Mon-Fri and 08:15–12:30 Sat; Gozo's main post office is in Republic Street, Victoria, with the same opening hours. Stamps are also available from newsagents in some towns and villages.

Internet cafés can be found in the main tourist areas of Malta and Gozo.

Electricity
The power supply is 240 volts, single phase, 50 cycles. Standard (UK) rectangular three-pin plugs are needed.

Weights and Measures
Malta uses the metric system for all measurements.

Health Services
There are two general hospitals in the islands: St Luke's at Gwardamanġa, near Valletta, tel: 2124 1251; and Gozo General hospital in Gozo, tel: 2156 1600. There are also health clinics in several towns and villages. Pharmacies are open Mon–Sat from 08:30–13:00 and 16:00–19:00; on Sun one pharmacy per district opens in the morning from 09:00–12:00 on a roster listed in the newspapers (or call the Police HQ, tel: 2122 4001). Most hotels have the services of a doctor on call. In emergency, tel: 196. Malta has reciprocal health agreements with several countries, including the United Kingdom and Australia. Visitors from both countries receive free medical treatment for the first 30 days of their stay.

Health Precautions
There are no health risks when travelling to Malta, though visitors should have full medical and travel insurance in case they require further treatment or medical evacuation. Visitors to Malta need no inoculations, but should take care with the strong sun.

Emergencies
Dial police 191 (general inquiries, tel: 2122 4001), ambulance 196 and fire 199. There are police stations in most villages.

GOOD READING

Attard, Joseph. *Britain and Malta – The Story of an Era*. Publishers Enterprises Group, Malta.

Blouet, Brian. *The Story of Malta*. Progress Press, Malta.

Bradford, Ernle. *The Great Siege – Malta 1565*. Penguin Books, London.

Bradford, Ernle. *Siege of Malta 1940/1943*. Penguin Books, London.

Gerada, Eric & Zuber, Chris. *Malta – An Island Republic*. Editions Delroisse.

Monsarrat, Nicholas. *The Kappillan of Malta*. Pan, London.

Ross, Geoffrey Aquilina. *Images of Malta*. Miranda Publications, Malta.

Schermerhorn, E. W. *Malta of the Knights*. AMS Press, New York.

Etiquette
As Malta is a strongly religious country, visitors to the islands' cathedrals and churches should dress accordingly. Men should ideally wear long trousers rather than shorts (though this is rarely, if ever, enforced); women should cover their shoulders (a wrap may be available at the church door) and avoid wearing shorts or miniskirt. Topless bathing is against the law.

Language
While Malti is the national language, English is widely spoken and understood, particularly in the resorts.

INDEX

Note: Numbers in **bold** indicate photographs